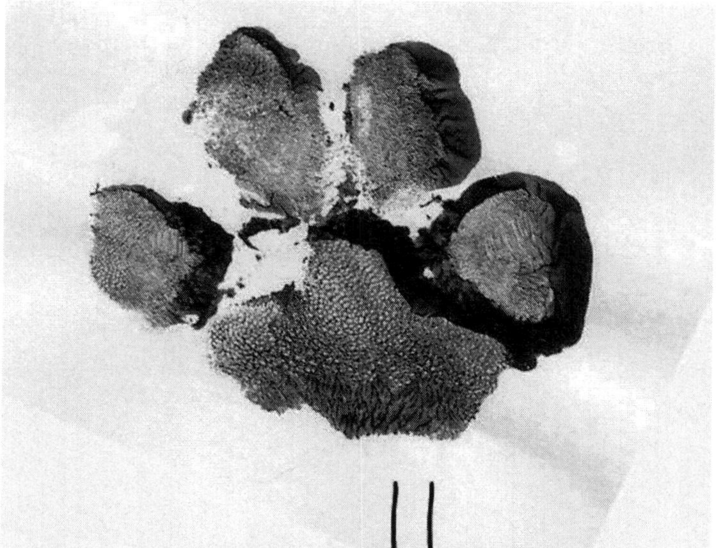
sally

Life With Sally

Waggin' More Tails

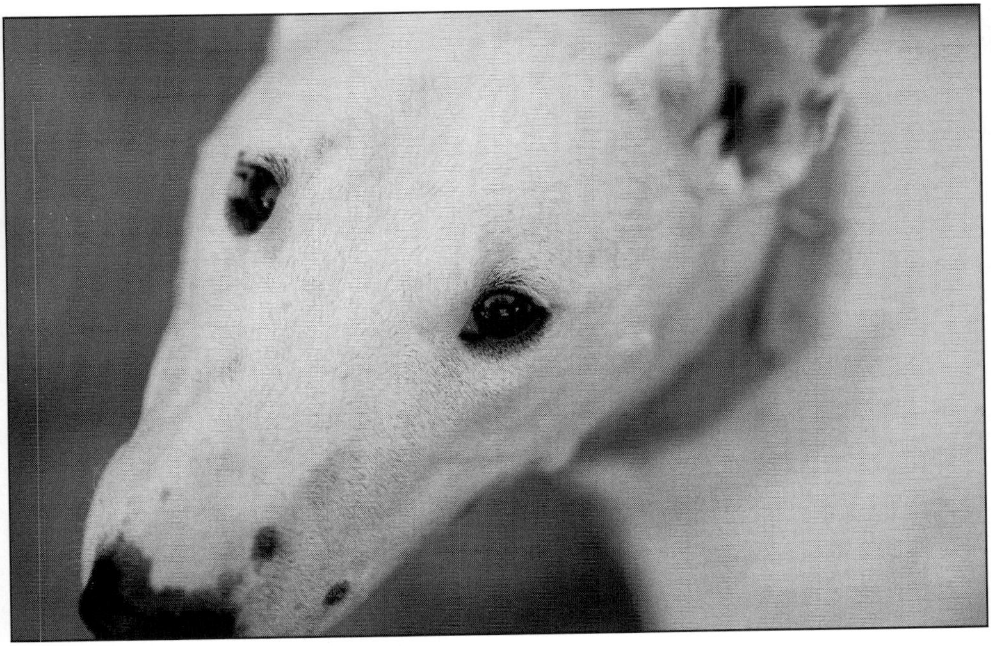

by

Tricia L. McDonald

Life With Sally
Waggin' More Tails

Cover design by Jacob Kubon

Cover and title page photos by Blink Photo

Published by

splattered ink press

splatteredinkpress.com

ISBN 978-1-939294-20-3

SALLY

As always –

this book is dedicated to my muse

… Sally.

Acknowledgments

First, I want to start by thanking Sally for providing me with so many stories. Without her crazy antics, the Life With Sally series would be very, very boring.

Thank you to Sally's fans. I am always excited to hear from people who enjoy reading about my dog. Thank you for loving this little girl.

My son, Jacob, created the incredible cover for this book. I love it when he tells me to trust him when it comes to the cover – I do and it is always fantastic.

Thank you to my daughter, Nicole, for being so involved with the formatting and editing. I love that we are able to work together on this book.

And Mike, my husband, who just shakes his head at Sally and I, but then says, "Sounds like a story."

My writing groups and friends should be sick of hearing me read the Sally stories, but instead they provide me with fantastic feedback and suggestions.

Finally, thank you to everyone who has sent me an email or taken the time to tell me how much they enjoy reading about Sally. That keeps me writing!

Table of Contents

Quirky or Crazy?

To say Sally is a bit quirky when it comes to eating her food would be an understatement, although it's not entirely true. She isn't so quirky about eating, but she is quirky about what she eats her food out of.

When we got her as a puppy, we fed her out of small matching ceramic bowls. She didn't seem to have any problems with the bowls and never hesitated when it came time to eat. If we moved them, there was a problem. So we never moved them. Problem solved.

As she got bigger, the bowls became too small for her ever-growing snout, and I noticed she was eating out of the side of her mouth. She had to turn her head sideways to get her tongue in the bowl so she could get the food. It was quite the feat, but didn't seem like a good idea. So, I got new bowls. In fact, I bought matching bowls that came in their own little stand. I put Mary's (our lab/cocker mix) in front of her, filled the bowls with food and water. No problem.

I put the bowls down in front of Sally, and she backed away. I filled them with food and water, and she stayed where she was, away from the dishes. I coaxed her forward by holding food in my hand above the bowl. Didn't work. I held my hand in front of her, and she nibbled at the food. I moved my hand toward the bowl again, and she backed away even further.

"Sally, you either eat out of these bowls, or you're going to go hungry," I said. Within a few days of coaxing, begging, scolding and pretty much pulling my hair, I put back the old dishes, and she dove right in. Quirky.

When we moved into our new house, we had to find places for the dog dishes. I put Mary's on one side of the kitchen, Eli (our jack Russell/Australian cattle dog) on the other, and Sally in the laundry room right off the kitchen. Perfect. Everyone seemed okay with this arrangement.

It was going so well, in fact, that I tried the new bowls for Sally again. No go. She still refused to eat out of them. I even bought new bowls, but she wouldn't eat out of those, either. So we were back to the old ones, and she seemed fine.

After a little bit, however, Sally stopped eating altogether. What was going on now? We checked to make sure she wasn't sick – no, she was okay. We hadn't changed the type of food, so that wasn't the problem.

I moved the bowls. Nope. I tried a different type of food. Nope. How about moving the mat under the bowls? Nope. She would eat out of my hand, but I put my foot down and refused to feed her that way. Well, I did let her eat out of my hand a few times, but only when no one was home to see me.

Out of exasperation one day, I picked up her bowls and dumped the food onto the red and white checkered mat that sat under the bowls. Tada! Sally ran over and dove right into the pile of kibble. What? That's it?

I washed the bowls, put them in the cupboard and ever since we have fed her off the mat. It took a little convincing to get Mike to agree to this arrangement, but after he failed at getting her to eat out of her bowl; he gave in, as well. Life with little Miss Quirky was happy again.

There was some initial concern about her water bowl, which she also refused to drink out of, but we did notice she would drink out of Eli or Mary's dishes. Until lately.

Behind our house, we have a very large pond. When we let Sally outside, she heads down there and wanders around the pond looking for amphibians or sloshing through the mud. She won't swim, but she will wade for hours. And of course, she drinks the water out of the pond.

For about a month or so, Sally was barking at the door to go outside even though she did not have to "take care of business" and we couldn't understand what she was up to. Then I watched her as she ran directly down to the pond and started drinking. After that it was obvious she was refusing to drink out of the bowls at home, but she would drink out of the giant water bowl in the backyard.

"Watch her," I said to Mike when he opened the door and let her outside.

She ran halfway down the driveway, turned right through the perennial garden, over the short wall, across the backyard and to the edge of the pond. With both front paws standing in the water, she started lapping.

"She's crazy," Mike said.

"Quirky," I said.

"Look at her, Tricia. She's crazy."

I watched as Sally stopped drinking and started racing around the pond.

"Well, maybe a little crazy," I said. "But mostly quirky."

Magic Mesh Mania

The sun shines in a baby blue sky void of clouds and the wind creates soft ripples in the pond. I sit at the desk in my office and look out the French doors at this idyllic scene. *What a great place to write,* I think. The door is open, and a warm breeze floats through the screen.

I turn back to my computer and my fingers tap on the keys, filling the blank page on my monitor with words. I am transported to the world of an imaginary couple, Joe and Maude, who are characters in my latest manuscript. I have fallen in love with them and find myself laughing out loud at their antics.

I am jerked back to reality by the sound of dog nails scratching at the door screen.

"Mary, no," I say before I even look up. I know it is Mary because she is the screen destroyer. Since we moved into this house two months ago, she has torn 15 window screens. Fifteen screens! It seems that every time we leave and come back, we find at least one or two screens with large holes in them. Can you say separation anxiety?

After she jumped out of a two-story window, we now close all of them before we leave the house. Somehow she didn't injure her 13-year-old body with the fall, but the thought of what might have happened changed our routine. Closing the windows protects her, but since the screens are on the inside of the windows, it doesn't protect the screens.

I spin around in my chair and sure enough, Mary has one paw on the screen as she looks at me. "Bad girl." I walk over, open the door and she runs outside. Sally bounces off my legs as she dashes out, with Eli close behind her.

Mary finds a spot of shade under a small maple tree and curls into the lawn. A grasshopper leaps into the air and Eli follows it across the yard. Sally is walking along the edge of the pond, stopping to stick her long snout into the mud on occasion.

I go back to my desk and Joe and Maude. Leaving the door open about a foot, the dogs come in and out, always within my view. The hours pass and I get a fair amount of writing done. The dogs have tired themselves out, no unwanted bugs have discovered the open access to my office and I consider the day a success. Thus, a routine is established, and the open door becomes an everyday occurrence.

One morning, I am engrossed in the words forming on my computer screen when a butterfly glides through the open door. There are butterfly bushes blooming in various shades of purple outside my window filled with butterflies for the past week. I jump to my feet, startling the dogs napping in various places around my office. Eli spies the butterfly, leaps onto a chair and stands against the back of it trying to reach the insect. Sally hides behind the door and Mary looks confused. I push myself between Eli and the struggling butterfly, cup it into my hands and release it outside. I close the door, and we go upstairs for lunch.

Back in my office later that day, Mary is outside napping and Sally is making her way around the pond again. Her white body is stark against the greens of trees, shrubs and grasses growing along the edge of the water. Eli is sleeping under my desk. Black feathers burst through the open door, and I flinch.

"Oh no," I scream, caught off guard by the small bird that has somehow found its way inside. *How am I going to get it back outside?* As this thought enters my mind, the bird turns and flies back outside. I sigh a huge breath of relief and relax back into my chair. *Maybe the open door isn't such a good idea.*

As I walk toward the door, I see Eli under the desk. His eyes are the size of saucers as he peeks out at me.

"That scared me, too, Eli," I say. He creeps out as I call Mary and Sally to come inside. That is the end of the open door for that day.

That evening I am channel surfing when I see an infomercial about Magic Mesh door cover. It is a screen that attaches to the outside frame of a door. There is a split down the middle that allows easy access but then closes (magically) with the use of magnets. Plus, if I buy one, I get another one free. *Perfect!* I throw the remote onto the couch and run to the kitchen for paper and a pencil. The next morning I go online and order a Magic Mesh door cover. I really don't need two, but I'm sure I can come up with a use for the free one. *The doggy door into the garage!* Sally won't use that door unless it is taped open. Leaving it open defeats the purpose so she won't use it.

The magic mesh will work perfect for the office door.

Unless, of course, the little white dog is afraid of magical mesh.

Eli Loves Linens

I wrote the first Life With Sally article in April of 2007, over six years ago. That means I have written 77 stories about Sally, or maybe I should say she has provided me with 77 topics. Although on occasion I have struggled with ideas, Sally always manages to do something entertaining for me to write about. However, there had been times when I struggled a bit for a topic. The month of October is not too difficult because I know if I pull out Halloween costumes, something is bound to happen, and I am often right. She was not happy with the idea of dressing as a banana and shared that displeasure with me.

This month is another story, and I continue to struggle. Sally is not what I would consider a normal dog, and for that I am happy. Think about how hard it would be to write month after month about a normal dog. No, she has provided me with licking toads, playing with 6-foot garden rakes, hunting butterflies, obsessing over our cat Louis, and many more escapades. But tonight, as I sit here with my fingers on the keyboard, I start to wonder if maybe we are done with the Sally stories. She is lying beside me; her snout tucked under her paw, and snoring. In other words, not doing anything too exciting.

Eli is on the couch watching me, and there is plenty I could write about him right now. He was on a naughty-dog rampage all day. It started when he pooped and peed in the guest room this morning. Mind you, this was after he had been outside earlier and pooped and peed out there.

While I was cleaning up his mess, the UPS guy showed up, and Eli went on a barking frenzy. I headed toward the door and found the large entryway rug in disarray. It looked as if Eli had tried to drag it through the house, but got bored with the idea after about three feet. Plus, of the shoes sitting on the rug, one was missing.

In the bedroom, I found the missing shoe on the bed, along with a throw pillow that had been gutted. One corner had been ripped open, and stuffing was strewn across the bedspread. Oh, and the sheets had been pulled out from under the pillows. I'm sure that made it easier for Eli to suck on the edges of the pillowcases until they disintegrated. Since Eli became a member of our family, we have gone through at least a dozen pillowcases and numerous sheets. He seems to have a linen fetish.

"You know, Sally is like a perfect dog," I say to Mike. I stroke Sally's ears.

Mike looks at me over the newspaper he is reading and smirks. "Why would you ever say that?"

"Well, she doesn't poop or pee in the house; she doesn't chew on shoes and she doesn't destroy sheets and pillows." I fill him in on Eli's escapades for the day. Eli is keeping an eye on me as I talk.

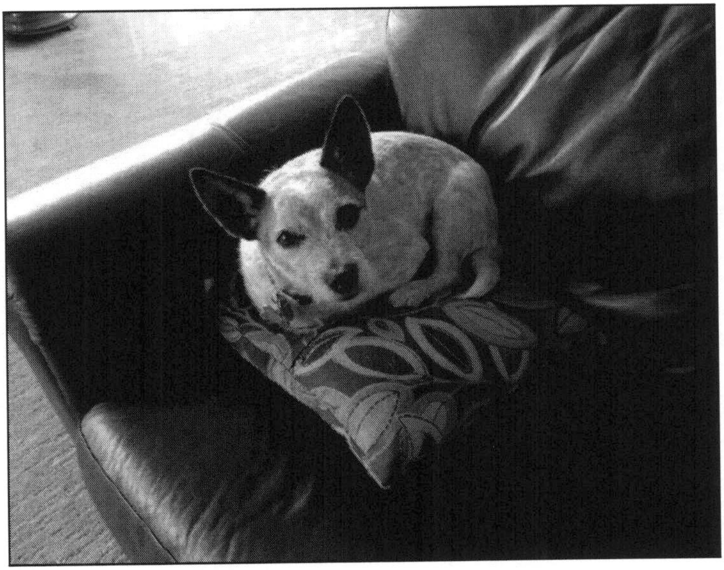

"He just gets bored," Mike says.

"Bored?" I say. "I'm sure the princess gets bored too, but she has never been that destructive."

"Right, she just finds a toad to lick."

I choose to ignore him and head to the bathroom to get ready for bed. Sally follows me but stops at the doorway.

"Come on, Sal," I say. She takes a tentative step forward and then scuttles backward.

"What's the matter with her?" Mike asks.

"I'm not sure," I say as I look around the room. "Oh, that's the problem." I pick up a box from the floor beside the bedroom door, and Sally trots past me. "She didn't like where the box was sitting."

"You're right, that's a normal dog," Mike says, sarcasm dripping off each word.

"I didn't say normal, I said perfect."

Sally jumps onto the bed and snuggles down into the pillows. I give her a kiss on the head and go into the bathroom. After washing my face and completing my before-bedtime routine, I grab my pajamas. Putting one leg inside, I find the pant leg is gone. All that remains are a few tatters of material.

"Eli!!!" I yell.

Sally's First Day of Kindergarten

I wait for the rain to stop, and then Sally and I make a dash for the front door of Bauerwood Elementary. Once inside, there is a flurry of activity as locker doors slam and voices call to one another.

After signing in, we start down the hall toward Mrs. Korpi's classroom. Sally pulls at her leash until we hit the linoleum floor, and then her paws slip and slide while she tries to get traction. When I lean down to pick her up, my neck scarf falls across my face, blinding me. I whip the scarf over my shoulders, startling Sally, and she leaps forward, jerking on her leash and almost pulling me off my feet. At last, I have my scarf in place and my feet planted on the floor. As I pick up the little white dog, I groan as I arrange her in my arms. She seems to have put on a bit of weight since the last time I held her.

At the door, Mrs. Korpi greets me, and I tell her that Sally gets nervous if a lot of kids rush up to her. The teacher goes into the room and I hear her talking to the students in a soft, calming voice.

When we enter, five-year-old Addie is standing at the front of the room. She drops to her knees, holds out her arms and Sally wiggle with excitement.

"Sally," Addie says. I put the little white dog on the carpeted floor and she barrels into Addie, knocking her back onto her butt. She giggles while trying to pet Sally who is still wiggling, with an occasional spin thrown in, and trying to lick Addie's face. The children in the classroom are laughing, but staying seated on the floor in a large half circle.

Addie (Addison Cumings), is the daughter of our friends, Tim and Jaci, and today is her day for show and tell. Her wish was that Sally could visit her class. She and Sally seem to have formed a special bond when Addie was a baby and they adore each other.

I sit on the floor with Sally, and Addie sits in a large rocking chair beside us. Mrs. Korpi asks Addie to tell the class about her special guests.

"This is Sally," Addie says. She leans down to give Sally a hug, and Sally jumps up at her.

Addie loses her balance and slides out of the chair. "I love her," she says.

She goes on to talk more about Sally and even mentions me, once. Then she asks if anyone has any questions. Little arms fly into the air and Addie points to individual children for their questions.

"Ummm, Sally's cute," one little boy says.

"Thank you," Addie says. She looks at me and nods. I smile. "Say thank you, Tricia," she whispers behind her hand.

"Thank you," I say.

The questions continue and Addie answers each one. She fidgets in the rocking chair while listening to their questions and I make sure I say thank you at the appropriate times.

Sally wanders around me, sniffing at the various items near us. She stands against the rocking chair again and when Addie bends down to kiss her; Sally bangs her long white snout on Addie's nose. She jerks back and I see tears fill her eyes.

"Are you okay, honey?" I ask. I have been on the receiving end of that snout many times, so I know how it can hurt. She nods, rubs her nose and the tears disappear.

"Can we pet her?" a little girl asks.

"Would you be afraid if a bunch of dogs, all bigger than you, came rushing up and started licking you?" I ask. There are wide-eyes and nods.

"That would be scaaary," a little girl says.

""Well, that's how Sally feels when lots of children come running up to her. She gets a little nervous," I say. "So if you come up one at a time to pet Sally, then she won't be afraid."

Sally has wound her way around me several times and tangled me in her leash. Addie is leading Sally in the opposite direction attempting to untangle me. The children laugh as the leash tangles around Addie. She makes a face, shakes her head and sits back down on the rocking chair.

I pull Sally into my lap and kiss her head. Addie invites each child, by name, up to pet Sally.

After everyone has had a chance to pet her, we say our good-byes and the children wave and thank us for coming.

Out in the hallway, Sally spots the outside door and starts dragging me toward it. She is slipping and sliding but doesn't seem to notice the slippery floor as she makes a beeline toward freedom. It is pouring rain, and of course, my umbrella is in the car, but the little white dog is squirming and pawing at the door so I open it. She runs out, squats and I can almost hear her sigh as she pees. Once she is done, she does a full-body Sally shake, and starts running.

Together, we dash through the downpour and every mud puddle on purpose, just like kindergarteners.

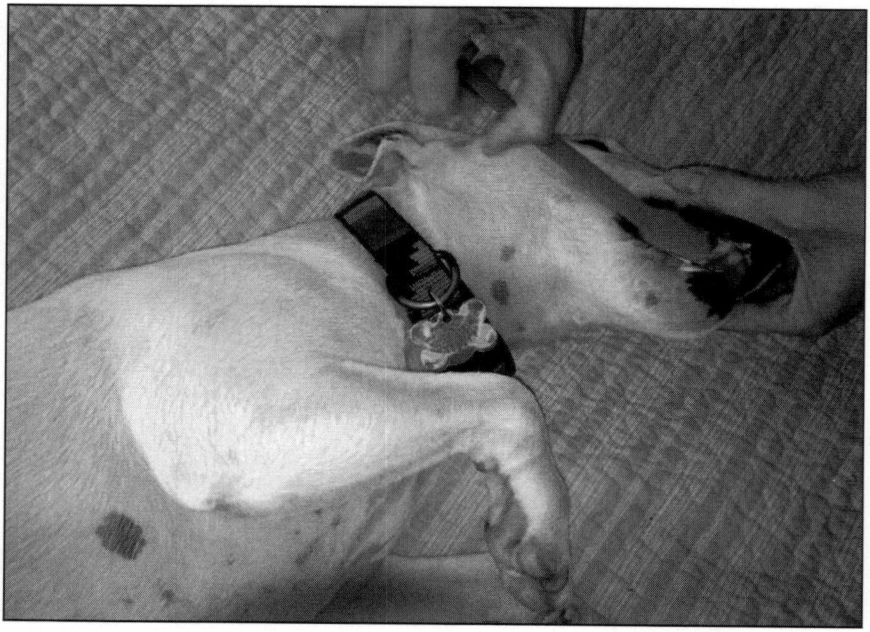

Keepin' the Pearlies Pearly

You have to do what?” my husband asks.

“Brush Sally’s teeth,” I say. I massage Sally’s ear as she lies on my lap in the living room.

“Good luck with that,” he says.

“Sally's doggy dentist said brushing her teeth would be the best preventative to keep them from getting so gross.”

“Tricia, you know that is never going to happen, right?” He ruffles Sally’s head. “She is not going to let you get anywhere near her with a toothbrush.”

“I’ve been working with her,” I say. Truth is, it has not been going well. I haven’t even been able to massage her gums (step two) without her running away from me. However, I’m not ready to claim defeat, yet. “And tomorrow I’m going to try the toothbrush." I say this with conviction, almost convincing myself. I would try it right now, but I don't think I want an audience.

The next afternoon, while the dogs are lounging in various locations in the living room, I walk into the kitchen where the doggy treats and toothbrush paraphernalia are kept. Sally follows behind me and when I reach into the cupboard, she starts spinning. Eli rushes in and slides across the hardwood floor, bumping into her. I grab the toothbrush and smear a glob of chicken flavored toothpaste across the bristles.

"Sit," I say. They both sit and look at me with serious intent. Mary is still asleep on her pillow in the living room, so I do not wake her. I give Sally and Eli a treat, and then reach for Sally's face. She must think I have another treat in my hand so she opens her mouth. Eli sees her open mouth and my hand, so he pushes in between us. I hold the toothbrush over my head and away from both of them.

"No, move Eli," I say. I nudge him out of the way with my elbow and kneel on the rug in front of Sally. I reach for her mouth again and she backs away. I crawl toward her on my knees, and she continues backing up.

Eli sneaks up and licks my face. I am about to scold him when he looks up at me with his soulful brown eyes.

"You're a good boy, Eli, but you're not helping the situation. Go lay down." I wipe at the spit on my cheek with the hand holding the toothbrush and now have chicken flavored toothpaste on my eyebrows.

Sally is sitting across the room on her haunches and Eli is licking his lips, staring at my eyebrow.

I can hear Mary snoring in the other room. I put more paste on the toothbrush and head toward Sally on my knees, which is not very comfortable since I am now off the rug and on the hardwood floor. I hold the brush out in front of me toward Sally.

"Come on, Sal, treat." She walks toward me, tail wagging, and I can feel victory just a few inches away. She hesitates so I reach for her collar to pull her a little closer, but lose my balance and fall toward her. She backs up too fast and her paws start slipping on the floor. Her legs are moving but her body is staying in one spot, while I am trying to keep the toothbrush out of my hair.

Eli decides to make his move and snatches the toothbrush from my hand and dashes to his kennel. Sally gets traction, follows him into the bedroom and runs under the bed. I am on my hands and knees shaking my head, when Mary saunters over to me and licks at the toothpaste in my hair.

Later that night, Mike picks the toothbrush off the counter and looks at me. I hold up my hand, palm open toward him.

"Don't ask," I say.

He chuckles and puts it back down.

"Defeated?" he asks.

"It would appear that way." I walk into the bedroom and sit next to Sally on the bed. She is lying on her side and I pet her ears and her face.

"Why won't you let me brush your teeth, Sal?" I rub her nose and lift her muzzle. She doesn't move, so I rub my finger along her teeth.

Again, no movement.

Back in the kitchen, I grab the toothbrush, smear it with the chicken flavored toothpaste and go back and sit by Sally. As I hold the brush by her face, she licks at it and then lets me rub it along her teeth. Her tongue is working like mad trying to get all the paste off, but victory is at hand.

"Good girl, Sal, good girl." I run into the living room holding the toothbrush high in the air like a scepter. Sally follows behind me.

"No way," Mike says.

"Way!"

A Frosty Morning

"Okay guys, let's go outside and take care of business," I say as I open the door. Mary, Sally and Eli jostle their way out, bouncing off my legs. I follow behind, pulling my bathrobe tight around my body against the blowing snow and below freezing temperature. I must be quite the sight in my winter boots, ratty bathrobe and bed-head hair. Thank goodness our house is sheltered by trees.

The tree limbs are heavy with thick snow weighing down the branches and only two tire tracks on the long driveway are visible from when Mike left hours ago.

"Come on, Eli, take care of business." He is the dawdler and will ignore his bladder if we don't keep after him. He stops by a bush and lifts his leg, then puts it back down without doing anything and heads toward the door.

"Nice try, buddy," I say. "Now take care of it for real this time." He starts to lift his leg against the porch beam. "Uh, uh. Now get out there." He wanders over to a tree and this time he does pee.

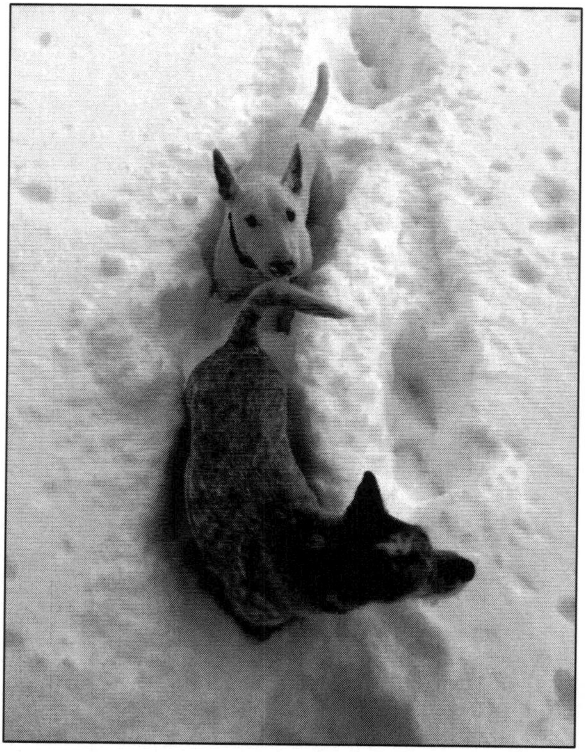

Sally wanders down the driveway a bit when a deer bursts out of the orchard and runs in front of her and into the woods. The fur on Sally's back stands up and she hops up and down in one spot. On the down she takes off running after it.

"Sally, no," I yell.

Eli hasn't seen the deer, thank goodness, because I know he would chase it and not stop. Sally isn't that adventuresome or courageous. She is standing at the edge of the woods, peering between the trees with timidity.

"Sally, come here." She looks at me, back at the woods, gives one bark, and runs toward the house, stopping to squat and pee.

I turn my attention to Mary who is heading down the driveway away from the house.

"Mare," I yell. She is losing her hearing and only hears certain pitches. I guess the sound of my voice when I screech "Mare" is one she hears. Of course that doesn't always mean she pays attention to it, and this is one of those times. She continues down the driveway.

We live in the woods with a very long driveway that empties out onto a private two-track road. I'm not concerned about her getting hurt on the road, but I don't want her wandering off.

I step off the porch into the snowfall. "Mare," I try again. She stops and I breathe a sigh of relief. The last thing I want to do is chase her down the driveway in my bathrobe. She turns and looks at me as I clap my hands. "Come on, sweetie."

I wave my arms in the air trying to get her attention, since her eyesight is getting worse, also. I know she sees me because she wags her tail and then, she turns and trots back down the driveway. I start trudging after her and Eli runs ahead of me.

"No, Eli, back to the house." I point toward the front porch, but he must see something move in the woods because he takes off like a shot, snow flying up around him. I hope the deer isn't lingering.

"Eli, get back here."

Now Mary has turned the corner at the pole barn and I can no longer see her. The snow is so deep it is over the tops of my boots and my bare feet are now wet. I mutter as I try to walk in the tire tracks, hoping that will help keep additional snow from falling in my boots.

"Eli, come here. Eli!" I can hear the bell on his collar, but I can't see him through the trees. I consider calling Mary again, but I know she won't hear me so why waste my breath, since every time I open my mouth I can see my breath in the cold air.

I round the pole barn and look around. No Mary. I squint and peer into the woods. Nothing. Looking at the ground, I see her tracks continue down the drive, so I walk in that direction. I stop and listen for her bell and hear a soft tinkling. It gets louder and she emerges from the trees running and bouncing in sheer doggy joy. I would smile except my toes are freezing. She runs past me and toward the house.

One down, two to go. I turn around and with daylight rising, can make out the shape of Eli just inside the tree line.

"Come on, Eli, let's go." He bursts out of the woods and chases Mary to the house. I hobble along, searching for the little white dog that blends in with snow.

A movement to the left catches my eye and I see snow flying into the air in short bursts. Eli sees it, too, gives chase and pounces ... on Sally. The two of them start scrapping in the deep snow, chasing each other, then stopping to wrestle, then back to chasing.

The snow is coming down harder now and my glasses are speckled. I take them off and try to wipe them on my bathrobe, but of course that is wet as well.

"Come on, you chuckleheads, let's get in the house." I look up and see Mary sitting on the porch, waiting for us. Sally and Eli fly by me as one, and I lose my balance, performing a ballerina pirouette before landing on my butt. I stand up and continue toward the house, my teeth chattering.

I open the door and the three amigos run inside, shaking snow off their coats. If only I could do that. Mary drops to the floor, pulls snowballs off her paws and Eli eats them. Sally shakes so hard she loses her balance and falls over, then pops back up like a jack-in-the-box.

I kick off my boots, shed my soaked bath-robe and jump back into bed to warm up. I curl my shivering body under the blankets, with only the top of my head exposed. A wet nose nudges the blankets and I lift my arms. Sally wiggles underneath and snuggles up next to me ... with her cold, wet body.

The Fishy Pied Piper

"Come on guys," I say. "Let's go outside."

I stand aside as all three dogs blast through the open door. You would think they were never allowed outside by their exuberance. But I think it is just the unexpected warm sunny weather on a March day that has them excited. I know it has me excited.

Sally chases Eli across the yard, and then they change direction and Eli chases Sally. Often Sally is hopping on three legs as Eli has her fourth leg in his mouth. There is never a mark and she never yips so I know he is not hurting her, but it is a little disconcerting to watch.

Mary has found a sunspot and is rolling on her back in the grass. My first instinct is to yell at her to get up because that usually means she has found something dead or gross. Today I decide that after being cooped up in the house, a little grossness on her fur won't hurt.

I head off down the path on the left side of the lake. "Let's go, chuckleheads," I yell and they all run toward me. Eli bursts ahead and Sally runs down to the water and starts lapping. She continues lapping and lapping and lapping. I expect to see the water level drop with all the drinking she is doing. However, I also know that when she drinks not a lot gets into her mouth. I don't understand this, but after mopping up lots of water around the dish in the kitchen, I know it to be true.

I raise my face toward the sun and soak in the warmth of a spring day, even though it isn't spring yet. A 70-degree day in March? In Michigan? Crazy, but wonderful.

Mary is pooping in the woods and I see Eli sneaking up behind her. I know this look and it means he thinks Mary is leaving him a snack. Dogs can be so gross.

"Eli, no!" He stops, looks at me and continues toward her. "Eli, don't you dare. Come over here you gross little bubba." He sprints toward me for some lovin', and then we continue our walk. The distraction works, this time.

I look around for the Sal-Mal and see her walking along the shore of the lake. She is actually in the lake, which is always surprising based on how hard I tried to get her into water in the past. Now all of a sudden, she loves wading.

I walk to the edge of the lake and call her to me. She starts to run, then splashes herself and stops, blinking.

"Come on," I say. She starts out again, this time walking with very deliberate steps and I'm sure it is to avoid splashing. I reach down to pet her, my foot slips on the wet leaves, and now I'm standing in the lake on one leg. Of course, my downward slide has freaked Sally out and she takes off running, splashing both of us.

She steps in a hole in the lake and is now up to her belly in water. By the look of fright in her eyes, she is not happy. Eli has heard the commotion and is standing at the top of the embankment looking at me. Mary is barking. It is doggy pandemonium.

I climb back up to the path and coax Sally to me. After giving her some lovin' and shaking my wet foot, we head off to complete our walk. A movement in the water catches my eye and I stop to look. Five black shapes are swimming close to where Sally and I were just standing. I look closer and see five large bass.

"Hooray," I say out loud. "They didn't die." We shut off the bubbler during winter and the pond froze over. We were concerned the fish would die, but decided dead fish were better than dead dogs. By the size of the fish, it is obvious they not only lived but also thrived.

I run back to the house, grab a handful of fish food pellets and dash back to the lake. Sally is back in the water and when I look closer, I see all five fish swimming within a foot of her. She doesn't seem to notice them. I toss some food in for them and they ignore it. They don't even come to the surface of the lake to check it out. They just ignore it!

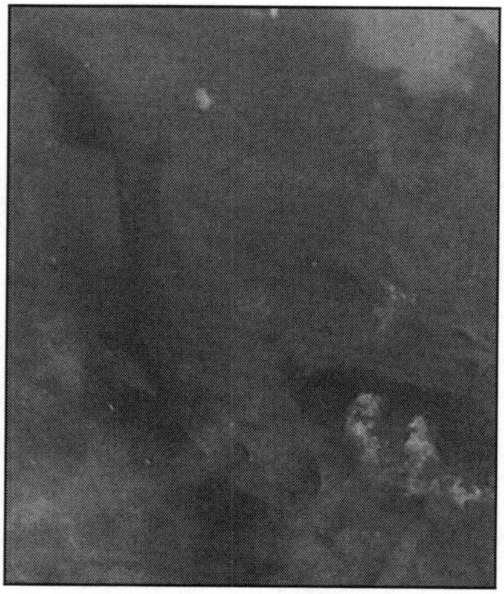

"Hey, stupid fish." I throw the food right at them and again, they don't even look at it. The little white dog, however, is eyeing the pellets floating on the water. She steps closer, and the fish don't swim away from her. Sally dips her head toward the food, grabs a couple in her mouth and sputters. It is obvious she got water in her nose.

"Come on, Sal. Let's get out of here." We continue our trip around the lake, and I see the fish following Sally, the fishy pied piper, as she makes her trek through the water.

Is Anyone Working?

I work out of my home, which is wonderful, except I have three interrupters – Mary, Sally and Eli. Therefore, instead of just going into my office and working, a routine must be followed so I am not interrupted every few minutes.

First, everyone outside to pee. Myself not included.

"Come on you knuckleheads, everybody outside." Eli runs to a bush; Sally darts to the kennel area, and Mary squats alongside the driveway. Next, we take a walk around the lake, and finally, when we get back to the house, I shake the treat jar and they run inside.

Everyone is fed; we have gone for a long walk, and they have taken care of their business, so I go to work. Mary follows me downstairs to my office, Eli and Sally head to the bedroom for a snooze.

Sitting at my desk for about 10 minutes, I notice Mary is pacing. I drag her pillow from the TV room into my office and she curls twice, then drops. A few minutes later, she decides to give herself a bath and the sound of her licking is making me crazy.

"Mare, please stop." She looks at me, wags her tail and lays down her head.

After 30 minutes of uninterrupted work, I hear a thump followed by a loud scrabbling noise from upstairs – the sound of doggy toenails on hardwood floors. Sally starts barking, Eli joins in and by the location of the noise, I know they are standing at the front door. Mary is still sleeping on her pillow. Losing her hearing has benefits.

I head upstairs to see who is here, my obvious assumption since the dogs are making such a ruckus. My movement wakes Mary. She dashes ahead of me and now she is barking, too.

"Guys, guys," I say at the top step. "I get it, someone is here." I look out the window, but there is no one in the driveway. I open the door and the dogs run outside, then stop and look around. No one.

"Okay, dummies, take care of business." I might as well make use of this interruption in some constructive manner.

Everyone follows me back down to my office, where Mary lies on her pillow and Eli lies next to it. Sally stands looking outside at the pond. I sit down and open the document I have been working on. Sally barks; Mary leaps up and I jump.

"Sally, quit." Mary joins her at the window and Eli takes this opportunity to sneak onto the doggy pillow. Returning, Mary stands and gives him the evil doggy eye.

I turn back to my computer and resume typing. Sally bumps my arm with her snout, and my fingers hit the wrong keys. Grrrr! I keep typing. She bumps me again.

"Sally, you have been outside twice and had a treat. Now lie down and leave me alone." She hangs her head and looks at me with just the top of her eyes. The look doesn't work this time and I go back to my computer, but she doesn't give up that easily. Another bump with the snout and I swivel in my chair. "No, Sally." She sulks off.

After a few minutes of work, the quiet worries me. I'm a mother; I know silence is often not golden. I glance around and see Eli sleeping in the middle of the pillow; Mary sleeping on the edge of the pillow, and Sally sleeping on the floor behind my chair. Breathing a quiet sigh of relief, I put my fingers back on the keyboard.

My excitement is short-lived when there is a bump on my shins. I scootch my chair back and see Sally's beady little eyes staring at me from under my desk. How did she get there? Has she become a Houdini-dog?

"Forget about it, Sal." Her snout drops onto my knees. I ignore it. The snout does not give up and starts pushing against my legs. I continue to ignore her. Sort of. It is almost impossible to ignore the little pest so it would be more accurate to say I do not respond.

BAM! She tries to stand up on my legs and bumps her brick-like head against the keyboard under the desktop.

"Oh, poor Sally. Are you okay?" I push my chair back and she takes this opportunity to rest her chin on the chair between my knees and gives me the sad eyes look. Of course, it works.

"Okay, you win. Let's go outside." She backs out from under the desk and starts spinning. Eli leaps off the pillow and Mary sits up, blinking her eyes.

Work will have to wait.

Saying Goodbye to Mary

This column is dedicated to Mary.

"Are you sure?" Mike asks as he walks in the bedroom, tears filling his eyes. I sit on the bed with Mary and rub a spot behind her ears.

She makes a purring sound and pushes herself further into my hand.

"I'm sure," I say, as I choke on the words.

It is Friday and 30 minutes before our veterinarian is coming over to put our sweet little Mary to sleep. We have made this agonizing decision after months of watching her health, both mental and physical, deteriorate. And now the actual time is almost here.

Almost 14 years earlier, my children, Nicole (now 26) and Jake (now 24) saw an ad in the newspaper for free puppies. When we got to the house, we went to the backyard and were greeted by six yellow lab puppies. They were tripping over themselves with excitement and I wasn't sure how we were going to decide on just one. The owners told us the mother was a lab and the father was a cocker spaniel, but all these puppies looked like their mother.

Jake was sitting on the deck steps when a little reddish-colored paw reached out and started playing with his shoelace. Pretty soon the paw was followed by a body with wavy fur, similar to a cocker-spaniel, with the sweetest little face. That was all it took, as she made our decision for us.

In the car, our sweet little hiding-under-the-porch puppy howled. All the way home, she whimpered and no amount of snuggling quieted her down until we got out of the car. Then she was quiet and full of spunk.

We had recently seen the movie Napoleon so we decided that would be his name. Notice I said 'his' because at the time we thought she was a he. Later that evening we realized he was a she, and so began our life with Mary.

When Mike and I married about a year later, we moved in with Harry, Mike's Border terrier. Harry was a 'Mike-dog' and only tolerated the rest of us, but on occasion he would play with this Mary-puppy who had invaded his space. After Harry passed away five years later, Mary would walk to the end of our driveway and lay down every day for hours. She was grieving her buddy and even her beautiful red fur took on a dull appearance.

Then along came Sally and there were times when Mary would give me a look like, "Where did you find this crazy little thing and does she have to stay?"

She and Sally never became playmates, but Mary perked up and her depression went away. The years passed and her muzzle became whiter, her eyes took on a milky glaze and when we called her she didn't always hear us.

The worst for Mary, and us, was her increasing anxiety. She had always been a bit of a Nervous-Nelly, but now we worried she might hurt herself. Our windows had screens on the inside and when we left, she would tear at the screens, trying to escape. She only tore at the open windows, but one evening we forgot to shut a window when we went to bed and she tore the screen apart and fell out of a two-story window. She wasn't hurt, but when we found her she was standing in the backyard, wild-eyed with fear.

Within a week of putting the screens in the windows this year, she destroyed 16 of them. All those windows had been closed. I just couldn't imagine the stress she had been feeling to tear at those screens.

In the last year, she had become my office buddy and would nap on her doggy bed beside my desk while I worked. However, if she woke and I wasn't there, she would panic and pace through every room until she found me. When medication didn't help, we made the difficult decision that she couldn't continue this way.

The doorbell rings, Mary jumps off the bed and runs to the door, barking one last time. Dr. Jolee has arrived and it is time to say good-bye. We put Sally and Eli in the garage, while Mike and I sit on the bed with Mary. I give her a kiss from Nicole and Jake who came home the week-end before and spent extra time with her. We caress her ears, whisper love as the vet adminis-ters the medication and Mary takes her last breath.

Later, Dave from Sleepy Hollow arrives to take her body to their crematorium. He carries a beautiful wicker basket lined with plush red velvet. Mike lays Mary inside; we tuck a tennis ball and one of Jake's old t-shirts in with her. I give her a last snuggle and she is gone.

Thank you sweet girl, for fourteen years of the best kind of love – unconditional.

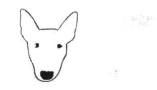

Toad Licker Extraordinaire

"Come on guys, let's go for a walk," I say. As soon as the word "walk" is out of my mouth, Eli bails out of his kennel and Sally starts spinning like a top. They collide as they run for the door and I stand still until they get past me, afraid they will crash into me if I don't.

I open the door and stand aside as they rush out. The skies are overcast and threaten rain, but the air is warm. I have my flowered knee-high water boots on so I can walk the edge of the pond and look for frogs, turtles, minnows and anything else brave enough to stay in the path of me and the little white dog.

The dogs tear down to the water and start lapping. There is always a bowl of clean fresh water in the house, but they seem to prefer the pond water full of who-knows-what. I continue around the north end and soon a white blur runs past. Sally hits the pond full blast and then slows to a walk as she makes her way ahead of me.

I know something is amiss when she stops and starts dipping her head in and out of the water at a crazy pace.

"Sally, what are you doing?"

Her head is swiveling and bobbing up and down, up and down. When I get closer to her, I see it. Or rather, I see them. Toads. Lots of toads. And the little toad licker is in heaven. I can almost see the smile on her goofy little face as she dips her head toward one toad and then another jumps and she swings around to that one.

I have never seen so many toads in one place before. At first, I think they are frogs because they are in the pond, but then I remember toads lay their eggs in water and I see the long strands of eggs floating under the surface. Sally doesn't seem interested in the eggs, only the little amphibians.

I move up the bank so I don't step on any of them. One hops about a foot ahead of Sally and she follows it into the pond, dips her whole head underwater, and then comes up snorting water out of her nose.

"Sally, you're crazy," I say aloud. Eli is not interested in the toads so he and I continue our walk. The little white dog stays right where she is, surrounded by her obsession. I keep an eye on her but she doesn't move more than a few feet either way of the toad infestation.

It starts to rain and we head to the house. The 'we' is Eli and I, as Sally doesn't seem to notice the weather has changed.

"Come on, Sal." She doesn't move. "Come on, crazy girl. Let's go in the house." There is no acknowledgment that she even hears my voice.
I run into the house, kick off my boots and grab a towel to dry myself. In the living room, I look out the window for the little toad hunter. And there she is, in the same spot, in the pouring rain, chasing toads. Eli jumps onto the chair beside me, looks out the window, and then up at me. "I know Eli; she's a little crazy sometimes."
I sit next to him and we watch her together.

Every time she drops her face toward the ground, shakes her head as if she is trying to get a bad taste out of her mouth, I know she has just licked a toad. And she does this over and over and over.

When the rain slows, I grab an umbrella and open the door.

"Come on, Eli, let's go get Miss Craziness." Eli gives me his 'Are you nuts? I'm not going outside' look and curls into a ball on the chair.

I tromp over to Sally. "Come on Sal, let's go in the house." She jumps at my voice, looks up at me startled, and then it's back to the toads. I try another angle. "Let's go get a treat." I turn toward the house and pat my leg. Nothing.

"Sally, your dad's home! Let's go!" She doesn't even look at me. "How about some suppies?" I'm sure that will get her attention, as she loves her suppies. It doesn't.

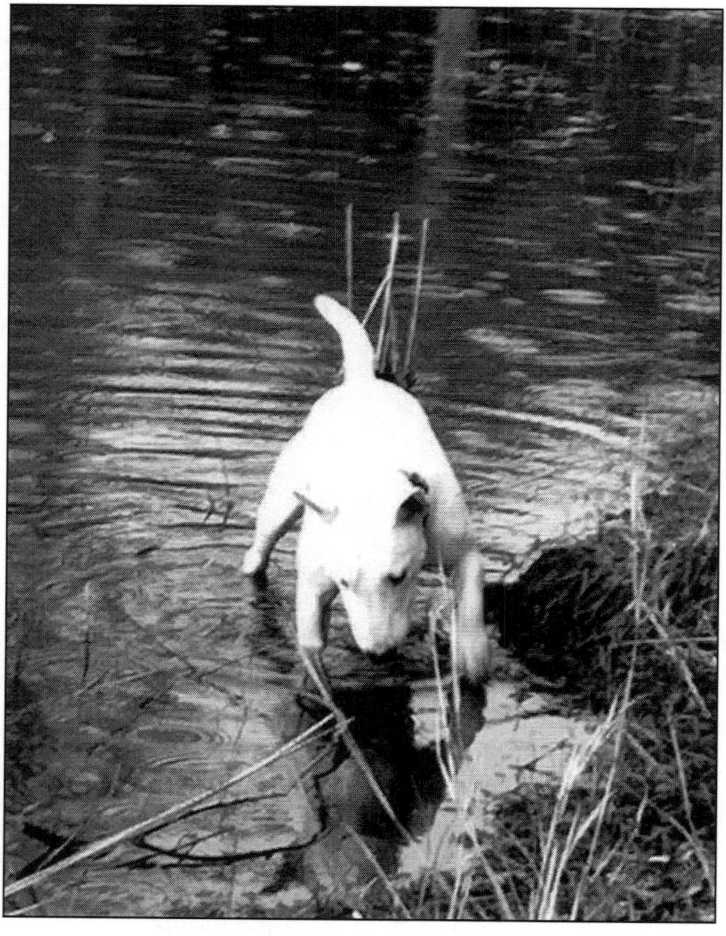

The raindrops are coming down harder, so I tug at her collar, but even that isn't going to take her away from what must be her dream come true – a plethora of toads.

I hoist her water-soaked body into my arms, pick up the umbrella and trudge to the house. Once inside I attempt to dry her off, but she is too wiggly and I let her go. She barrels onto the chair with Eli and stands against the back, staring out the window.

I can almost hear the toads heave a sigh of relief.

The Princess Appearance

Sally is straining at her leash as she and I walk into the Deltaplex in Grand Rapids for her appearance at the PetExpo. The place has a circus-like atmosphere with people of every size and age milling around, some pushing strollers and others walking dogs. I'm sure that at Sally's level, it is a sea of legs, wheels and the occasional furry creature. The noise is an overwhelming mix of voices, barking, and piped in music. My nose is assaulted with the smell of popcorn, sweat and animal urine. Sally's nose is up in the air immediately as I navigate her to our booth. Once there, she goes crazy on Janet (the editor of Cats and Dogs Magazine) for a few minutes and then checks out the floor for popcorn kernels.

"Look, its Sally," a young boy says.

She starts spinning in her happy-crazy way and I pick her up and walk to the front of the booth. Soon there are lots of hands reaching toward her, trying to give her touches. When the crowd dissipates, I walk back inside the booth and put her down. She is a heavy 25 pounds and my arms start aching after holding her for a bit.

She wanders around sniffing until more people come to see her and I pick her up again. I have tried walking her out to the front of the booth so people can pet her, but she gets nervous and tries to hide behind my legs. This ends up with her leash wrapping around my legs and presents a precarious situation for my well-being. In other words, it becomes an excellent opportunity for me to fall on my butt. So instead, I hoist her into my arms and she is happier.

More people come by and we repeat the picking up, petting process, but now Sally isn't her happy, wiggling self as she is stressed and tucks her nose into my armpit. When I put her down, she hides under the table, peeking out from under the tablecloth. I reach down to pick her up again, and she backs away from me so I have to crawl underneath to reach her.

There is an unexpected lull in the crowds so I leave Sally with Janet and go to the concession stand. For the next half hour or so, Janet, Sally and I munch on popcorn in between fans coming by to see the little white dog celebrity.

Sally gets perky and we take turns tossing popcorn into her mouth. She doesn't catch much, but does a good job of keeping the floor clean.

The vendor next to us has a myriad of pet paraphernalia, so I buy a yellow doggie raincoat and put it on her. We laugh; she does not appear to be amused.

I sit in a chair by the opening of the booth and hold her on my lap so people walking by can pet her, and she won't stress out. This works until a gaggle of little kids come running toward us, and she almost backs off the chair. I stand and hold her so they can at least touch her paws.

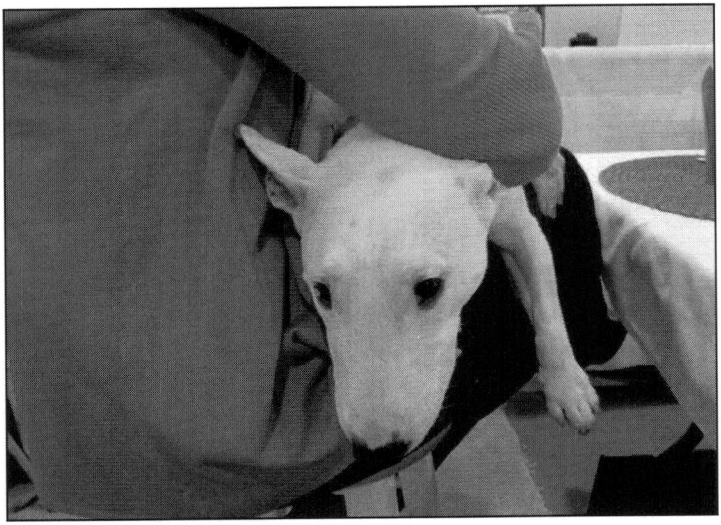

The clock ticks by and soon her two-hour appearance is over and she gets to go home. When my sister, Joyce, appears, Sally must know she is the ticket out of there because she starts banging into Joyce's shins.

"What's the matter with her?" Joyce asks, rubbing her leg.

"She is so ready to get out of here," I say.

"Poor Sally," Janet says. "When she gets here she is so excited, but by the time she leaves she is exhausted."

I walk Sally out to Joyce's car, buckle her into the seatbelt and give her a kiss between her ears as she settles into the seat.

Joyce calls me an hour later to let me know they made it home okay.

"Sally was asleep before we even got out of the parking lot," she says.

"Well," I say, "it must be exhausting to be a diva."

I'm a Dog - Not a Banana!

"Come here, Sal," I say as I walk into the house. I drop the shopping bags on the counter and a banana doggy costume falls onto the floor. Sally runs over and shoves it around the room with her long white snout.

"That's your new Halloween costume, Sally," I say. Now Eli is sniffing at the yellow material and I snatch it away from the two of them. The last thing I need is a doggy tug-of-war over a banana costume. Halloween is not that far away and it is the only time I can get away with putting clothes on Sally without everyone groaning. Everyone being my husband Mike and my kids, Nicole and Jake. But come to think of it, even at Halloween they groan.

I pull an orange tiger costume out of a bag and, along with the banana, hold both of them in front of Sally.

"What do you think, Sal? Do you want to be a tiger or a banana?"

Sally looks past me and must spot the open door because she darts right outside. I guess she's not as excited about this process as I am at the moment.

"Okay, Sally, let's go for a walk first," I say. "Come on Eli, let's go outside."

He streaks by me and bangs into Sally, knocking her sideways. She boomerangs back at him with her rock-hard head and he side-steps. They zigzag across the lawn, bouncing off one another as they make their way down to the lake. I smile at their antics until I see Sally run to the water and then I remember ... mud! Black, stinky, messy mud. The water is so low this summer there is deep mud all along the edge.

"Sally, no!" She looks back at me and then continues lapping at the water. By the time I reach her it is too late. She is up to her tummy in mud and this is not conducive for trying on costumes. "Ugh!"

I find doggy treats in my pockets and manage to entice her away from the water (and mud) and back up to the front door.

"Stay," I say as I wrestle with the hose and sprayer. She stands in one spot, but gives me the 'you're killing me' look as I spray off all four paws, legs, tummy and myself in the process. I spray a little longer than necessary, mistaking some of her black skin spots as dirt. I let go of her and turn off the nozzle as she gives a Sally shake – it starts from her nose and goes all the way to the tip of her tail, lifting her off her feet. I meet her at the door and with two towels, get her dry enough to go inside and start the Halloween fashion show.

Eli, during all of this, has been standing stone-still watching for mice in the garage. For the past month, every time he runs into the house and directly to his kennel, I worry that I'm going to find a mouse in there with him. So far, no mice.

"Come on Eli, no more mouse hunting for today." I open the door and he and Sally bolt past me. Well, Eli bolts past me. Sally bolts onto the rug just inside the door, stops and drops to her belly, looks across the room at our bedroom (where there is carpet), and then tippy-toes across the wood floor until she hits the carpet. She slips on the wooden floors so everywhere she goes in the house is determined by where there are carpets and rugs.

Grabbing the costumes, we head into the living room and I start wrestling the tiger costume around Sally's white body. It takes extra wrestling as it appears her belly is a bit more rotund than it used to be. I can relate.

Eli wanders over to see what we are doing, Sally chases him away and the tiger lies in a heap on the floor. I pick it up and turn Eli into the tiger. He sulks over to the fireplace hearth and watches from a distance.

"Okay Sally, one down and one to go," I say as I grab the banana costume. That too, is a snug fit but she wiggles into it and I put her on the couch for a photo shoot. I aim the camera at her, but she will only look straight ahead.

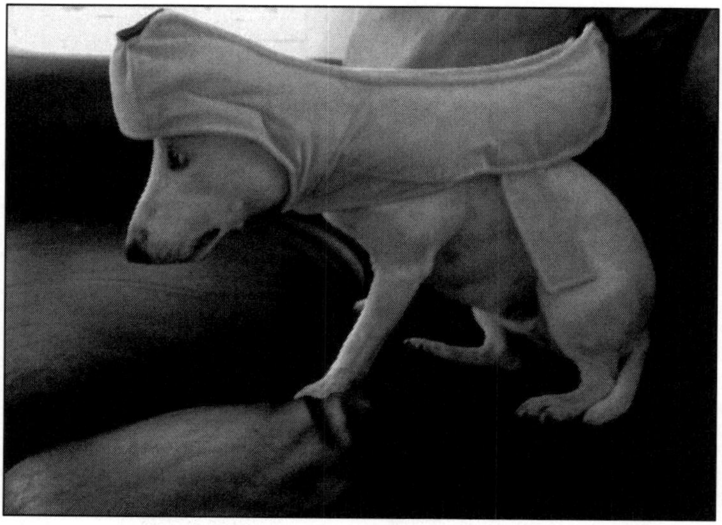

"Sally, sally, sally," I chant. She refuses to look at me and I start laughing. She turns her head in the opposite direction. Uh oh – it appears the little white dog is not happy.

Jumping off the couch, she rubs her body along the carpet in an apparent attempt to escape from the costume. Eli uses this opportunity to leave the safety of his ledge and investigate. Sally takes off after him and they run in a circle around the furniture. I am laughing so hard there are tears in my eyes. By the time they stop, the banana has slipped sideways on Sally's body and Eli has run right out of the back part of the tiger suit.

I wrestle Sally back into the tiger suit, but her enthusiasm for this costume show is waning.

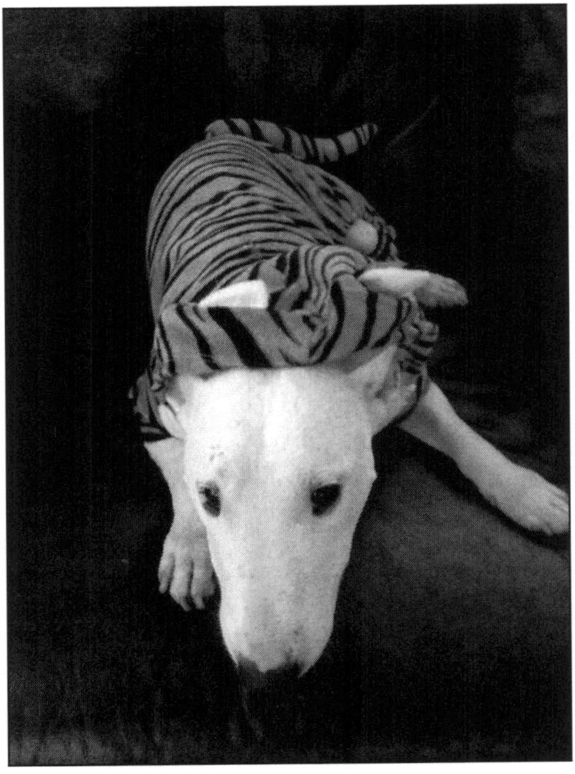

So I guess there won't be any dressing up for Halloween this year, but at least that means I won't have to listen to any groaning.

Sally Shadowing

"Sally!!!" I say, as Mike opens the back door. I squat and she barrels toward me, full blast, and I brace myself for her welcome. I have just arrived home after spending four days in New York and it is obvious Sally is happy to see me. She always makes coming home rewarding with her exuberant greeting.

She leaps against my legs until I sit on the ground and accept her kisses. Eli comes by to give me some face licks, but Sally isn't too interested in sharing me right now so she chases him off after a few quick kisses.

In the house, I sit on the couch and chat with Mike about the trip. Sally is spinning like a dervish in front of me. She spins and spins and spins, gaining speed until she loses her balance and almost hits the end table. I think she is done when she sits, but then she starts chasing her tail while sitting on the floor.

"Sally, you're crazy," I say while laughing. Mike is shaking his head and Eli is sitting next to Mike keeping an eye on everyone.

Sally stops her floor spinning and jumps onto the couch next to me. I scratch her chin, but that isn't enough for this little dog. First she lies down on the blanket beside me, then she stretches her neck until her head is on my lap, then she creeps forward until her entire body is on me, and then she starts licking my face. I'm moving my head back and forth, trying to see Mike around Sally's big ole' head, but the licking continues. I grab her face between my hands and cover her long white snout with kisses. That seems to satisfy her for a few minutes.

It is evening and the long day is catching up with me so I drag my suitcase into the bedroom and open it on the bed. Sally stands beside it as I take items out and put my dirty clothes in a pile while I hang the clean ones. I chat with her while I unpack, but it seems that isn't enough. She stands in the middle of the pile, turns a few times, and then curls onto the clothes. She looks so cute and comfy I hate to disturb her, but need to finish so I can shower.

"Move, Sally," I say. She doesn't even raise her head. "Come on, move." Nothing. I pull the clothes out one at a time from under her, and she doesn't budge.

In the bathroom I am about to step into the shower when I hear her head banging against the door. I let her in and she follows me to the shower, but turns away when she gets splashed by water. She lies on the rug so I almost step on her when I get out. I sidestep and move to the sink to brush my teeth. It doesn't take long before she is lying on my feet. *Really, Sally?*

Dressed in my pj's and a comfy robe, I head to the kitchen for a glass of water. The little white dog shadows me from cupboard to sink to living room and then back up on the couch. This time she doesn't even pretend she is going to lie beside me. She is on my lap almost as soon as my butt hits the seat. She curls into a ball, closes her eyes and starts snoring. My eyes grow heavy and I rouse her to go to bed.

Another quick trip to the bathroom, with her shadowing me, and then I stand beside the bed tossing off the throw pillows.

"I see Eli had a munchfest with the pillows while I was gone," I say as I pick up a square brown pillow. All four corners have been chewed off and the white fluffy stuffing is starting to spill out. Eli is already laying in his kennel, peeking at me and I give him some kisses.

"I hated those pillows anyway," Mike says.

At last I snuggle under the blankets and Sally wiggles underneath. I roll onto my side and she walks up beside me. In one move, she drops her entire body against mine. I curl around her and close my eyes. Mike shuts off the light and there is a familiar stillness that settles in for the night.

"Good night, Mike," I say. "I'm glad I'm home."

"I'm glad you're home, too," he says.

Sally lets out a huge, loud sigh. I think she's glad I'm home, too.

She Is Not a Party Girl

Today is our yearly outdoor summer celebration and I am up early taking care of last minute details. Mike is working outside and I am putting together fruit and vegetable trays with my family. Sally is outside doing Sally stuff, like chasing down unsuspecting toads.

My son Jake and nephew Michel arrive with the new outdoor furniture and I run outside to help unload.

"Sally, no!" Mike says. He is raking the beach and the little white dog is grabbing the tines of the rake and jerking it away from him.

"Mom, where did you want this stuff?" Jake asks.

I look away from Mike and Sally. "Ummm, put the table at that end and ..."

"Tricia, call Sally," Mike says.

She has let go of the rake and Mike is holding it above the ground, but now she is spinning in a circle underneath, looking up and drooling.

"Sally, come here," I say. She keeps her eyes glued to the rake and doesn't even acknowledge her name. "Sally! No!" She turns her head toward me.

Mike starts raking again and she pounces. I march in her direction and she runs the opposite way. It is going to be a long Sally day.

Several hours later and everything is ready, including the sunny skies, and our guests start arriving. With no rake to chase, Sally is wandering around the yard looking for, what else, amphibians.

"Sallllllyyyyy," five-year-old Addie Cumings yells out as she runs into the backyard. Sally's head pops up and she runs toward her. Addie drops to her knees in the grass and Sally jumps all over her, licking Addie in every spot she can find. "Sally," Addie giggles. "Stop kissing me."

A few minutes later, other families arrive and soon there are six more little girls headed in Sally's direction. She is standing beside me and as the girls reach us, Sally backs into and around my legs. She stands behind my ankles as 12 little hands reach for her.

With short attention spans, the girls are distracted by something else and they run off in another direction. Sally is trembling as she wanders off the opposite way.

"Tricia, where's Sally?" Addie looks up at me. "I can't find her anywhere." It is about forty-five minutes later and Sally has disappeared.

"She's hiding in my closet," I say. "She gets a little nervous when there are a lot of kids around." Even without seeing her, I know that after the 12 hands incident, she made a beeline for my bedroom.

"She's not hiding from me, is she?" Addie's eyebrows knit together in a worried look.

"No, Addie," I say. "Sally loves you." And it's true. For some reason, Sally is different with Addie than she is with other children. As soon as Addie appears, Sally starts doing her happy spin, followed by lots of kisses on Addie's face.

"Can I go see her?" Addie asks.

I take her hand and we sneak upstairs into my bedroom.

"Sally?" I say as I turn on the closet light. A little white tail starts thumping and my blouses wiggle. "Come here, sweetie, its okay." I drop to my knees and Addie crouches beside me.

"Its okay, Sally. It's just me, Addie."

Sally creeps out from under the hanging clothes and Addie pats her on the head.

"I have to go back to the party," I say. "But you can stay here with Sally if you want."

Addie nods and rubs Sally's pink belly. "Sally, you're so silly."

I close the bedroom door on my way out to keep the other children out of the room. Sally needs a place where she feels she can get away from all the noise and excitement. My closet appears to be that spot.

After about an hour or so I realize I haven't seen Addie in awhile, so I head back to my room. Opening the door, I find the closet door closed and a step stool placed in front of it. Addie is crouched on the floor looking under my bed.

"I think she's ready to come outside," Addie says.

There is thumping and thudding and pretty soon Sally scoots out from under the bed. She stands and gives a full body shake.

"Come on, Sal, let's go outside," I say.

I open the bedroom door to the sound of little girl shrieks, Sally turns and bangs her head into the closed closet door. I open it and she bolts back under the clothes.

"Maybe she's not ready," Addie says.

I nod and take Addie's hand as we leave Sally alone in the closet. It appears the little white dog is never going to be a party animal.

Geese be Gone

Watching the activity on our pond is one of my favorite things to do in the morning, and today is no exception.

Out of the corner of my eye I see movement in the sky and with a big whoosh and a lot of honking, two Canadian geese land in the water. They float around for awhile and then walk onto our small beach. I love seeing the water fowl that visit our pond, but know that too many geese will result in a lot of goose poop in our yard and beach. And my concern isn't just with the mess, but also the fact that Sally and Eli will find their droppings a delicious snack. Gag!!

How can I get them out of here? I think. I look around the room and my eyes land on Eli, sleeping on a chair in the corner. With great stealth, I inch the sliding door and screen open onto our upper deck.

"Come here, Eli," I whisper. If I can get him onto the deck, he'll see the geese, start barking and they'll fly away. Eli lifts his head and looks at me. I'm not sure where Sally is or I would call her. "Eli," I say with more urgency. He continues to look at me, but makes no movement.

I hear a scrabbling noise and as I look around for the source, Sally crawls out from under the bed. She stands and gives her body a big shake.

"Come here, Sal," I say as I point out the door. She trots to the door and looks up at me. "Out, go out." She backs away and Eli continues to stare from his chair. I hear goose honking and see that the geese are now floating in the water again. This plan is not working.

"Let's go downstairs and outside," I say to the dogs as I close the doors. I slip my bare feet into my boots and tie the sash around my white terrycloth bathrobe a little tighter. The geese are in the middle of the pond and I imagine the burst of dogs barking and me running outside will be enough to scare them away.

I open the door and we rush outside. The geese start honking with more fervor and the dogs ... don't even look their way. Eli stops and looks up at me, I'm sure expecting a treat. Sally runs down the path around the pond.

"Really, you guys? Look." I point at the water. "Geese. Get 'em."

Nothing. Sally is now walking near the pond edge and the geese are moving toward her not away. *What? This is so not working.*

"Sally, look." She looks at me and I point at the geese, and for some unknown reason, at that moment she sees them. Of course the fact that they have floated to a spot almost directly in front of her may be the reason.

She jumps backward, loses her balance and lands on her little dog butt. She leaps back to attention and starts barking. *Finally!* She barks again and again. The geese honk back at her, but don't take off. In fact, they just turn and float toward the middle of the pond again.

I decide it is time for drastic action and I run toward the pond. My robe is flapping in the wind, my boots are stomping on the hard ground, and I'm screaming.

"Get out of here! Aaaaaggghhh!"

The geese don't move, but Sally takes one look at me and starts running in the opposite direction with her tail between her legs.

I trip on a tiny stump, start to fall and grab a nearby sapling to keep myself upright. Eli bumps into me because, of course, he has been herding me as I ran maniacally forward.

"Sally. It's okay, it's just me." She stops and looks my way. She gives her tail a slight (what I consider embarrassed) wag. The geese continue to float and honk at us. Sally hops toward the water and gives them a few more menacing barks, they continue to ignore her, and, did I mention it is hailing? I am getting drenched.

Our effort is fruitless. If the sight of a crazy-looking woman with a white garment flapping in the wind and yelling at the top of her lungs didn't scare the geese away, the barking of a little white dog is not going to move them either.

"Come on guys," I say to Eli and Sally. We turn back toward the house and they run ahead of me inside.

While in the bedroom changing out of my wet clothes, I hear Eli barking in the living room. He and Sally are standing on the chair in the corner, looking out the window and barking. I look out and, sure enough, there are the geese walking (and I'm sure, pooping) on the beach.

"Good job, guys. That's going to scare them away for sure." Of course, maybe they weren't trying to scare them away. Maybe they were thanking them for the outdoor snack.

Obsession #984
A Fake Toad

I was at a local landscaping/flower store when I walked down an aisle and was inundated with the sound of frogs croaking. Lining three shelves were 30 decorative outdoor frogs, each with an electronic eye in its mouth. When they sensed movement, they croaked.

How fun, I thought. I held myself back and only bought one, although the idea of a dozen hidden in various places along the path around the lake was tempting.

At home, I unpacked flats of flowers and carried them to various gardens in my yard. It was a beautiful, sunny day before the mosquitoes hatched, so I was smiling and quite happy.

I had already forgotten about the frog until I moved the final plant in the car and heard the unmistakable "ribbit!" Sally's head snapped up from the piece of bark she was examining in the driveway. I waved my hand in front of the frog and he croaked again. Sally headed toward me at a dead run and came close to colliding with my leg. Been there, done that, not enjoyable.

I grabbed the frog and headed down to the lake with Sally close on my heels. Eli didn't follow us once he realized he couldn't eat it.

I found a semi-secluded spot under a tree and nestled the frog in some dead leaves. I walked back and forth in front of it, and each time I heard "ribbit." Sally sniffed at it a few times and it croaked at her. She stepped back, cocked her head, and then nudged it with her nose. I grabbed it as it started tumbling down a slight incline toward the water.

"Sally, no." I moved it to a spot in front of a tree trunk to prevent any further nudging toward the lake.

But now when I walked in front of it, there was no sound. I was hoping the batteries weren't already dead, so I waved my hands by the mouth of the frog. "Ribbit!" That meant it was just too far from the path, but I needed a buffer between the frog and the water.

I decided that distracting Sally might help in my attempt to find the perfect froggy spot.

"Sally, go get the geese," I said, pointing to a spot on the other side of the lake. She stared at the frog in my hand. "How about a treat?" She didn't even blink at the treat word so I knew this was serious. She kept staring at the frog.

Desperate measures were necessary, so I walked to the house while Sally jumped up and down at the frog in my hand. I faked like I was throwing the frog in the house and once the little white dog was inside, I shut the door. I hurried back to the lake edge, found a spot in the dead leaves where I again semi-buried the frog. As I walked by, I heard the now familiar "ribbit!"

Several days later I was sitting on the deck when I heard Sally barking. Fearing the focus of her attention might be a deer; I dropped my book and jumped up to look. There she was, standing in front of my frog, and I could hear a faint "ribbit!" "ribbit!"

"Sally, leave the frog alone." I waved my hands and raised my voice, trying to get her attention. She would not take her eyes off the fake amphibian. She nosed it around the tree and the frog tumbled down the embankment and landed with a plop in the water. To my relief, it was floating and not sinking.

"Sally! Get that frog out of there!"

Sally inched into the water, grabbed the frog by the ear and backed onto the bank. She dropped it on the ground, gave herself a big shake, and then picked it up again and started trotting toward the house. The closer she got, the louder the "ribbit!"

I hurried downstairs and ran outside just as she was settling into the grass with her new toy. There was no licking involved with this frog as she started gnawing on it.

I grabbed it away from her and looking around for a safe place, decided to set it in the middle of a bird bath. Sally couldn't reach it, so it became a frog bath.

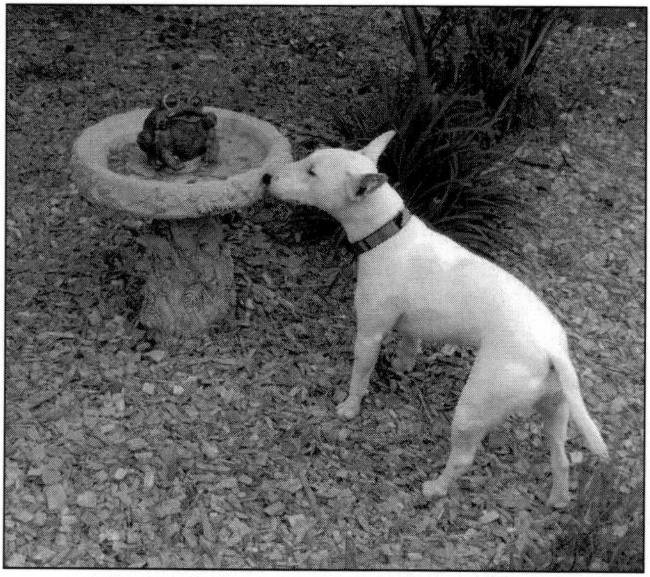

"Why is Sally so obsessed with that bird bath?" Mike asked me the next day. We were working in the garden and Sally was staring at the bird bath.

"It's got something to do with a croaking frog," I said, "but don't ask me for details. It's a long story."

Feeling Buggy

Sally was lying under the covers between Mike & me one morning and as I was rubbing her face I felt something small and hard.

"Is that a tick?" I said, grimacing.

"What?" Mike said.

"Is that a tick on Sally's face?"

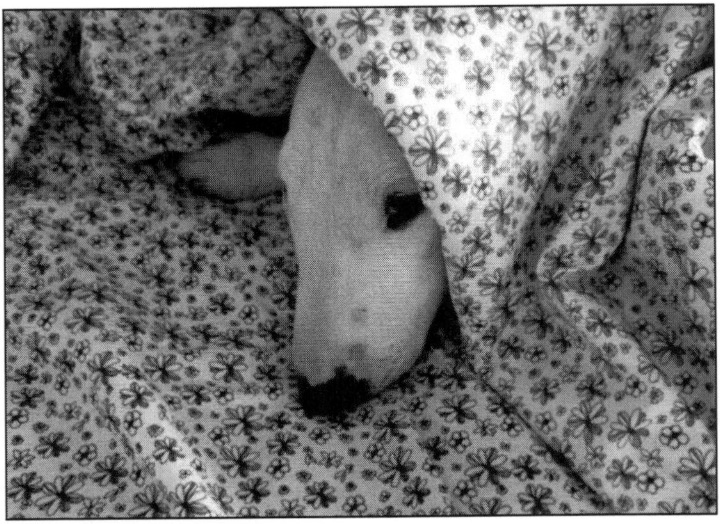

I threw back the covers and looked. Sure enough, there was a little black tick and it was getting ready to burrow into her skin.

I jumped out of bed, grabbed a tissue and snatched the nasty little bug off Sally and threw it into the toilet. Ugh! My body gave an involuntary shudder. I had been hearing and reading about the high incidence of tick sightings this year, but this was the first one I had seen.

Ticks give me the creepy crawlies. Several years ago I found a pretty big one attached right below Sally's ear. I was afraid to try taking it off myself, so I took her to our veterinarian's office. They had a nifty little tool made just for removing ticks and within a few seconds, it was off. I bought one of those tools and since then it has been sitting in a drawer. I hadn't even opened the package, but it looks like this may be the year I get it out and use it.

A couple weeks later, as I was getting dressed in the morning, I scratched my leg and felt a bug. I figured it was a mosquito, as they had arrived in swarms, and brushed at it but it didn't move. *What the heck?* I thought. As I looked down, I cringed when I recognized the black creepy little bug body. A tick! On me! As I was trying to remember where the tick remover was, the little critter moved and I could see he wasn't actually attached to my skin … yet. I tossed it into the toilet and did a little creepy-crawly dance.

"Mike, I just had a tick on me!" I said.

"Oh."

"Oh? Did you hear me? I said I had a tick on me."

"Okay."

"Ugh. It was probably on Sally and transferred over to me during the night."

"Maybe it was on me, then transferred to Sally and then crawled onto you," he said, smiling.

"You are a very funny man," I said, still cringing at the mere thought of the tick crawling on me.

Later that day we were all outside, after dousing ourselves with ample amounts of bug spray, and when I looked over at Sally she was covered in dots ... only these dots were mosquitoes.

"Sally!" I said as I ran toward her, waving my hands. This, of course, startled her and she stumbled backwards. Her sudden movement was successful in getting most of the bugs off, but I still managed to swat at a few of them.

The mosquitoes were so bad that even with bug spray on me, they swarmed around my face – trying to get in my nose and ears. Being outside was miserable, so we decided to invest in a bug zapper.

We checked around, compared models and prices, then made our purchase and brought it home. Mike took it out back and hung it along the edge of our property. We had high hopes that it would help with the mosquito problem, but it seems we were only adding to a little white dog's obsessions. You guessed it ... Sally and the bug zapper.

It started that evening, after dark. I was sitting in bed reading with a nice breeze floating in through the windows. Sally was lying next to me, after I had checked her over for ticks. Eli was on the doggy pillow on the floor. All of a sudden there was a loud zapping noise and, startled, I almost dropped my book. Sally started barking, Eli jumped up and ran to the French doors and looked out.

That bug must have been the size of a house. "It's okay, guys."

I went back to my book and the zapping continued ... and continued ... and continued. Each time, Sally would bark and Eli would run to the door. It was ridiculous. After reading the same paragraph three times, I gave up, put away my book, shut the door and the windows, and then the light.

In the morning, the dogs and I were sitting outside on the deck enjoying the beautiful weather.

At least, I was trying to enjoy myself. Sally and Eli were at the edge of the deck, staring at the dark blue glow of the bug zapper. And you guessed it ... every time it zapped, Sally would bark. Didn't bother me as much though, because I was enjoying a mosquito-free morning.

Which lasted for about 15 minutes ... until they found us.

Up the Stairs Down the Stairs

"What's the matter with Sally?" Jake asks me.

"Nothing, why?" I say.

"She won't come up the stairs."

"Oh, that's just her thing."

"Her thing? What thing?"

Our home is a bi-level, with our living area on the main floor. The lower level is our family room, my office, etc. The stairs are all open and you go down eight stairs to a landing, then turn to the left and go down another four stairs.

Sally is half-way down (or up, depending on your viewpoint) the main set of stairs and looking up at us. "Come on, Sal," I say.

She turns and goes down the stairs to the landing. There she turns around and starts running up again. Halfway up, she stops.

"You can't block the top of the stairs," I say to Jake.

"What? I'm just standing here."

"Yeah, but she gets a running start and has to make it up all in one smooth move. If she has to stop, she turns around, goes back down and has to start all over again."

Jake gives me a look that tells me he thinks I'm nuts, and then moves to the side.

"Come on, Sal," I say.

She goes back down to the landing, turns and starts back up again, then stops about three steps from the top.

"Now what?"

I look around the landing. "That's the problem," I say. I grab a bag that is hanging on the stair rail and move it to the kitchen with Jake following behind me.

"You know she's nuts, right?" Jake says.

"She has her idiosyncrasies." There is the sound of Sally's nails as they click, click, and click back down the stairs. "Just stay here where she can't see us," I whisper.

We stand still and within a few minutes I hear Sally as she makes her way up the stairs, one step at a time. Jake starts toward the stairway, but I hold up my hand in a stop motion.

"Wait until we hear her at the top," I whisper. "Otherwise, she'll start all over again"

"This is ridiculous," he says, as he shakes his head.

"Duh," I say. "Tell me something I don't know."

I peek around the corner just in time to see Sally reach the top step. She glances at me and stops. "Arrggghhh!"

"Come on Sally, let's go," Jake says as he walks past me. She turns and trips down the stairs, with him following close behind. On the landing, she stops and he picks her up. Carrying her to the top of the stairs, he sets her down on the hardwood floor where her paws start sliding.

"You need to put her down on the rug," I say. "Otherwise she gets too freaked out."

Jake raises his eyebrow at me. I've always wanted to be able to raise just one eyebrow at a time, but have never been able to master that feat. Jake is good at it and right now, his skill is irritating me.

At that moment, Mike pulls into the driveway and Eli runs past Sally and to the door. Sally tries to run, her paws slip on the floor, and she heads down the stairs again. She stops at the landing and looks up at us.

"That's it," Jake says as he walks away.

Mike enters the backdoor and Eli greets him with a fanfare of jumping, barking and licking.

"Hey Jake," Mike says. He looks around. "Where's Sal-mal?"

"She has an issue with the stairs," Jake says.

"What?"

"You knew that," I say.

Mike tries to raise an eyebrow, or at least that's what it looks like to me.

"She has a little OCD with regard to coming up the stairs," I say. "If she can't make it all in one run, then she will go back down."

"That's nuts," Mike says. Jake nods.

"Don't start with me," I say. "Either of you."

Sally's barking interrupts our conversation and we all move to the stairway and look down.

She stands on the bottom landing with one paw on the step, looking up at us.

"Come on, Sal," I say.

Mike and Jake walk away.

Vacation Planning

Preparing for vacation is the easy part. Getting everything arranged for Sally is the challenge.

Three months before vacation –

Sitting on the couch with Sally curled on my lap, I absently rub her ears. The fireplace is warming the living room and Eli is sprawled across the doggie pillow in front of the hearth.

"Hey, what are we going to do about the dogs while we're gone?" I ask Mike.

"Get someone to stay here."

"I know, but who?"

We go through the list of names of people we normally use, but most of them are no longer available.

"I'll ask Michel," I say. Michel is my nephew and has proven to be very dependable. Plus, I know he will let Sally sleep under the covers with him – even though he doesn't always admit to it. And the last time he stayed at the house, he texted photos to me which helped with my Sally withdrawal.

The next day I call Michel.

"Would you be able to stay with the dogs while we're on vacation?" I ask.

"Sure." Michel is a man of few words.

One month before vacation –

Sitting on the couch with Sally curled on my lap; I look out the window at the blizzard and think of our upcoming Mexican vacation.

"Hey, did I tell you Michel is going to stay here while we're gone?" I say to Mike.

"Hmmm," Mike says. We are watching one of those true life murder cases on TV and he is looking up more information on his iPad.

After 14 years of marriage, I know Mike is listening even though he isn't responding verbally. Unless a "hmmm" is considered a verbal response. And believe me, we've had that conversation.

"Michel will be gone all day on Monday through Thursday because of work, though," I say.

I rub Sally's belly and continue. "I'll check with a few people and see if I can find someone who does doggy sitting."

"Hmmm."

Three weeks before our vacation –

Sitting on a chair with Sally and Eli both laying on my lap, I look out the window at yet another blizzard and daydream about blue skies, hot weather and the ocean beach.

"Oh crap! I still have to find someone to stay with the dogs," I say.

Eli lifts his head and looks at me. Sally continues snoring.

Mike doesn't respond because he isn't even there. I'm starting to freak out.

Two weeks before our vacation –

Sitting on the couch with Sally on my lap and Eli stretched out beside me, I scratch Sally's ears and rub Eli's belly.

"Hey, did I tell you that Lauren came out today and met the dogs?" I say to Mike.

"Who's Lauren?"

"She's the college student who is going to take care of the dogs during the week while Michel is at work," I continue, now rubbing Sally's ears and scratching Eli's belly. "My friend

Patti gave me her name and highly recommended her."

"How did she seem with the dogs?"

"Great and of course they were jumping all over her like the not-well-trained dogs they are."

One week before our vacation –

"I need to make a doggy calendar for the week we're gone." I say to Mike.

"What?"

"I need to write up a doggy calendar so everyone knows who is supposed to be taking care of the dogs and when."

Mike turns onto his side. "Tricia, its 4:30 in the morning."

"I know. Did I tell you that Jake is going to help out too?"

A small purring snore is Mike's reply. Sally stands and shakes, then walks back under the covers and curls up behind my legs. Eli snuggles against my back, turning me into a doggy sandwich. I lay with my eyes wide open, listening to everyone sleep.

One day before our vacation –

Sally stands on a chair in the living room ignoring the suitcase on the floor, while Eli stares at it from the same chair.

"Michel is coming over tomorrow about an hour before we leave so we can go over the last minute details," I say to Mike.

"Good. Did you make your calendar?"

"Yeah. I printed out three copies so everyone has one – Lauren, Jake & Michel."

"Don't you think that's a little overkill?"

I ignore his comment.

Ten minutes after we leave for our vacation –

"Well, we're officially on vacation," Mike says as we drive toward Chicago. He takes my hand and kisses it.

"Do you think Sally is okay?" I ask. "She looked so sad when we drove out of the drive-way."

Mike rolls his eyes. "Go ahead," he says.

"What?

"You know what."

I send Michel a text.

Dogs Don't Do Drugs

As we drive away from the Bois Blanc cottage and head for home, I give the little white dog and her brother Eli, half of a doggy sedative prescribed by our veterinarian, wrapped in a piece of cheese. They love cheese and gobble it right down. Our thought is that the sedative will help them relax and sleep during the five to seven hour drive. We think this is a good idea.

Throughout the drive, I look into the backseat to check on Sally and her companion. Eli zonks out right away, but Sally does not. She has stopped chewing the harness, and is staring at me with very glazed eyes.

"Just close your eyes, Sal," I say.

"What is she doing?" Mike asks.

"She's just sitting there and staring at me, but her eyes do look sleepy." I reach back and give her a little lovin'. "It shouldn't take too much longer and she'll be snoozing."

Wrong! I look back at regular intervals and although she is wobbly, she is not going to close her eyes. In fact, she develops bug eyes. It is as if she is fighting the whole sleep idea and her wooziness is scaring her. I feel awful.

"Maybe she has to go to the bathroom," I say.

We stop at a rest area and Mike puts her in the grass. She takes a few unsteady steps, squats and falls over. Not good.

Eli does not wake up when Mike shuts off the truck, so I shake him a little.

"Eli, let's take care of business," I say. He does not budge. I reach in and pull him out of the truck. He is limp. I am really scared. I hold him like a baby, rub his tummy and ruffle his ears. "Wake up, Eli." Nothing. I have passed scared and am now moving toward terrified.

"Did Eli do his business?" Mike asks as he carries Sally back to the truck.

"I can't get him to wake up." My voice cracks and my eyes fill with tears. "I think there's something really wrong."

Mike pops Sally into the backseat and takes Eli from me. He holds him with his paws dangling just off the ground and Eli opens his eyes.

"Hey, buddy." Mike sets him onto the grass and Eli stretches. He takes a few steps, lifts his leg on the running board and pees. He does an unsteady body shake and heads back toward the truck door.

We settle everyone back in and continue on our journey. Eli falls back to sleep and Sally continues her staring.

"I thought we killed Eli," I whisper.

"Me, too." Mike adjusts the mirror, so he can see Sally. She stares at him with red-rimmed eyes. "Why doesn't she just go to sleep?"

"I think she feels too woozy to close her eyes."

"Jeesh, we can never give them a sedative again."

"Agreed."

I reach back and pat Eli. He opens one eye and peeks at me. All good. I pull Sally onto my lap, rub her ears and give her head kisses. She looks up at me, and then lays her head on my leg. In minutes, she is snoring.

"You don't think any of that eye-staring was just to get on my lap, do you?" I ask.

Mike looks at Sally snoozing in my lap. "What would give you that idea?" he says, raising his eyebrows. "She has to be the most spoiled dog in the world."

I bend down, give her a little kiss on her rock-like head, and she snuggles down deeper, keeping her crossed eyes closed.

They Make Matching Pajamas - Really?

Christmas morning and before I even opened my eyes I could smell the breath – and it wasn't good - of the little white dog. I opened my eyelids and there was her long snout lying on the pillow next to my face.

"Sally," I whispered. Her tail started wagging, puffing the blankets up and down.

I heard the second story kennel creak as Eli stood and stretched inside. Within a few seconds he was out of his sleepy-time-crate and onto our bed, licking me in the face. He is so quick with that little tongue of his that there has been more than one occasion where he got me on the lips. Ugh! But this time I heard him coming and was able to pull the blankets up over my mouth.

Sally wiggled her body out from under the covers and leaped onto Eli, and the two of them started doggy-wrestling between Mike and me.

"Hey buddy," Mike said as Eli darted around Sally, up to the pillow and stuck his paw on Mike's face.

"Merry Christmas, Mike," I said, shoving Sally's butt off my pillow and lifting my head so I could see him over the plethora of fur between the two of us.

Mike reached his hand in my direction, but Sally got to it first and started licking his fingers. At that point, we just gave up and got out of bed.

After potty breaks (for the dogs), feeding time (for the dogs) and another potty break (again, for the dogs) we gathered around the Christmas tree to open gifts. Jake (our son), had spent the night which was a treat for us since he lived in another town, but Nicole (our daughter) would not be able to join us in person again this year. She was living in New York and couldn't get the time away from work. I hated that! She would, however, be joining us via the telephone later in the day.

Sally had positioned herself in front of the presents and was not allowing Eli to come anywhere near. She had done the same thing last year, but then it was about only one present. This year she had expanded and decided that all the presents needed to be protected – from what, I'm not sure.

We went through the presents one by one, taking time to oooh and aaah, along with thanks and kisses. At last there was one present left for me from Mike. I tore open the gift wrap as I'm not one of those careful-to-save-the-paper-unwrappers. I just find an edge and rip into it, although with Mike's taping it isn't always easy to find an open edge.

At last the paper was off and I opened the box. Inside were flannel pink & white pajamas with little sheep characters on them. I was a little confused because I really don't wear flannel, but hey ... they were cute.

"Thanks, Mike," I said as I pulled the top and bottom out of the box. That's when another piece of the same fabric dropped into my lap. I picked it up and turned it over and over, trying to determine what it was. A head scarf? No. A matching slipper? No.

Sally, who had been sitting close to me, stood and sniffed at the garment. "What in the world is this ... oh my gosh." I started laughing and couldn't even finish my sentence. "No way!"

"What is it?" Jake asked.

"Matching pajamas for Sally," Mike said.

"Ridiculous." Jake shook his head.

I was lying on the floor and laughing so hard my stomach was starting to hurt. "I can't believe this."

"Try it on her," Mike said.

"Come here, Sal," I said. "Look at what I have." I sat up and wiped at the tears in my eyes.

I wrestled the soft material over her rock-like head and pulled it flat across her muscled back. She started walking away from me, then stopped and turned her head sideways trying to grab the pajamas off her. When this didn't work she rubbed against the couch. That didn't work either so she jumped onto the couch and started wiggling along the cushions.

Jake got up and took it off her. "There is something seriously wrong with you guys," he said, trying to hide his smile.

"You're just figuring that out?" I said.

Jake tossed the doggy pajamas at me and I folded them back into the box with mine and put it under the tree.

Later that night when I got ready for bed I put the toasty warm flannel sheep pajamas on and called Sally. She leapt onto the bed where I was waiting for her. I put the pjs on her and Mike took a photo before she had rubbed them off. I still wear mine on occasion but Sally refuses to wear hers.

I attempted to put them on Eli once, but he wasn't too keen on the idea. And at the time, I think I might have even heard Sally snicker.

I Wish It Would Rain

It is a beautiful day. The sun is shining, ducks are lining the banks of the pond, and I saw a doe and two fawns earlier in the morning. So it makes sense to go outside with the dogs and soak in the Michigan sunshine.

"Come on guys," I say, as I open the French doors. As I begin sliding the screen open, Sally becomes impatient and darts through my legs, knocking the screen off the track.

"Sally!" I grab at the door as it falls, banging onto the cement pad. The noise and quick movement startle the little white dog and she jumps into the air. When her paws hit the ground, she takes off running toward the pond.

I am too irritated to laugh at her because putting this door back into the tracks has proven difficult in the past, and yes, this has happened several times before. I should just call her Miss Impatient Sally.

Stepping outside, I turn to face the house with the door in my hand and I see Eli sneak by me and back inside. He must have slipped out while I was watching the princess. He runs past me and is headed for the upstairs on a quick run when my internal 'uh oh' kicks in. Whenever he makes a beeline for his kennel (which is upstairs), it is often because he has something in his mouth. Coming from outside, it could be anything - dead or alive. In the past we have found him with twigs, rocks, shoes, and once he even dragged the blanket off the bed and into his kennel.

"Eli, no!" I lean the screen against the doorframe and take off after him. He pauses and turns toward me. *Is that a tail hanging out of his mouth?*

"Eli, drop it." As soon as the words come out of my mouth I realize it could be disastrous if he does drop 'it' because then 'it' might be alive in my house. But I needn't have worried because Eli has no intention of dropping it. He darts past me and back outside. I chase him and on the way out, I bump against the screen and it falls over, bangs against the lawn chair and then onto the ground. Sally, who had been standing near it, tucks her tail between her legs and runs in the same direction of Eli. I run after the two of them.

Eli takes off into the woods just as I step onto a sharp object. A slow walk in the soft grass is great for bare feet and that was my intention when I first opened the door ... which seems like a long time ago. But a sprint across the grass and along the edge of the woods creates a plethora of danger to my toes.

I check the bottom of my foot for foreign objects, and then limp back to the door. After I get the screen back into the track, I go inside, sit down and put on my shoes. I try not to think about Eli and what he is doing at that moment. I do know he will not be giving me any face kisses in the near future.

After several minutes, Sally makes one of her strange, alien-sounding noises and I open the door and go outside. I give a quick glance around the yard, but do not see Eli the troublemaker.

"Eli!"

I see movement and notice him sitting across the yard, looking at me. It appears his mouth is empty. As I walk closer to him, he lies down and puts his chin on the ground. In front of him is a chipmunk, lying very still. As I lean in for a closer look, I see its tiny chest moving up and down. *It's alive!* Other than being covered in dog spit, it doesn't appear to have any outside injuries. I decide to get everyone inside and give the little fella a chance to catch its breath and get the heck out of here.

"Come on, Eli, let's go." I grab his collar and push him toward the house. He surprises me by running to the door. I sneak a peek behind us and see that the chipmunk is now sitting up. I look around for Sally and see her wiggling on her back in the grass. I smile as she jumps to her feet and runs to me.

The beautiful day may have started off a little rocky, but as I bend down to give Sally a hug, I take in a big, deep breath of the beautiful, fresh air. Immediately my nose wrinkles in disgust and I look around for the source of a horrific smell. *What is that?*

I start to pull the screen door open and Sally looks at me with the expectant 'treat' look, but Eli is sniffing at a dark spot on her side. It coincides with where I was just patting her and I lift my hand to my nose. "Ugh!" I gag a little.

Turns out, Sally wasn't wiggling on the ground for the sheer joy of feeling the grass tickling her skin. Oh no, she was rolling in something disgusting and now has the smell ground into her fur.

There is no way she can go into the house like this, so I push the door closed at the same time as Sally tries to dart inside. As she bangs into it, the door falls off the track – again. She jumps and falls against Eli, who ducks into a nearby bush.

I'm beginning to wish I had woken up to a rainy day.

Buckle Up, Sally

I open the passenger car door, and Sally slips by me and jumps inside. She tries to do a happy spin on the seat, but falls onto the floor. Recovering, she scoots over the console and into the back.

"Come here, Sal," I say, holding out her pink harness. She dives back to the front seat and I fit the harness onto her wiggling body. I buckle it into the seatbelt and we are off.

Sally is a pretty good passenger, if she is re-strained. If not, it is a game of backseat-front-seat-backseat-front-seat, which becomes annoying in about a second. As I drive to the assisted living center to visit my friend, John, I ply Sally with treats while she gives me the give-me-more stare.

John is not home, so our visit is cut short and I am left with a big decision. Do I take the princess back home and drop her off? Or, do I take her with me while I run errands? The last time I left her alone in the car, she chewed her harness in half and I was not happy.

I decide to chance it and take her along on the errands run. The first stop is a client's house to drop off marketing materials. I park in front of the house under a tree, roll all four windows down a couple inches, unbuckle Sally and head inside. I'm only gone a few minutes, and back in the car, I look around for damage. All seems good, so I buckle her in and we are on our way to the post office.

Luck is with me and I find a parking place right in front of the building, so I can keep an eye on the car while I am inside. Again, I unbuckle her, grab the 10 packages I need to mail, and off I go. Standing in line, I look out the window and see her staring out the passenger window. *Man she's cute!* And if she's looking out the window, I know she isn't causing bedlam, which makes her even cuter.

Two errands down and things are looking good. My last stop is the bakery. There are no parking places in front, so I have to park around the side of the building where there are no windows. I'm not crazy about this because I won't be able to see her, but she's been good so far and I take the chance.

Back in the car, I take a cursory look around and still don't see any Sally damage. I give her more treats and lots of loving. The errand running has been a success so far and I think I should take her with me more often. It's nice to have her company. I buckle her back in and we head for home. My last stop is my Mary Kay lady's house, which is less than a mile from home, so we are almost done.

A couple of blocks from my last destination, Sally has started wiggling and managed to tangle herself in her harness so she can't sit down. Since we're so close to home, I unbuckle her and she heads to the backseat where I hear her give a full body shake. The sun is shining, the sky is clear and blue, I'm leaving for a writing retreat in a few hours and I've spent the morning with little Sal. It's no surprise that I'm smiling.

I hear Sally's nails on the console and know she is heading back to the front seat and ... deer! Without warning, I see several deer out of the corner of my left eye and they are right at my front bumper. No way to miss them and all I see as we collide is Sally flying forward. My foot hits the brake, my right hand reaches for Sally, and the windshield wipers are on, the turning signal starts blinking, I see four deer in front and around me, then they are gone and the car has stopped. Sally is smashed up against the dashboard, although I do have a grip on her collar. Her nail is caught in the blower grill, and I gently unhook her and she jumps into the passenger seat. I do a cursory check and she doesn't seem to be hurt. I pull the car to the side of the road and get out. *What just happened?*

The front end doesn't look as bad as I expected, the tires are not flat, and there are no deer around. I get back in, and check Sally over again. Her only interest seems to be in the treats and I buckle her up. The car starts and I don't hear any strange noises from under the hood, so I drive off.

Should I really stop here? I pull into my Mary Kay lady's driveway. *Maybe I should just go straight home.* I sit for a minute and then decide to just get my stuff, as long as I'm already there.

"I just hit a deer," I say to Sue and Melissa as I walk inside.

"What? Are you okay?" Sue asks.

I hadn't even thought about whether or not I was hurt. I've just been worried about Sally.

"I think so." We talk for a few minutes, while I strive for normalcy, but while writing my check, I realize my hands are shaking as much as my insides.

At home, I let Sally out of the car and watch for any limping or unusual behavior, although with Sally that can mean normalcy. She seems fine and Eli greets us at the door with his usual excitement. I sit on the porch steps watching the dogs playing together knowing I will never unbuckle them while in the car again, and breathe in a sigh of relief. Then, my tears fall.

Sally's Village

It takes a village to raise a child, and I believe it has taken a village to care for Miss Sally, the little white dog. So, I would like to take this opportunity and thank those members of our village.

First and foremost, a HUGE thank you to my husband, Mike. He got the whole Sally ball rolling when he found her breeder. Once he showed me a photo of this tiny white puppy sitting at the bottom of a tree, I was focused on bringing her to our home. At the time, I thought she was going to be Mike's dog because I wasn't a dog person. Little did we know the little white dog had her own way, and it wasn't long before I was a Sally person.

Our dilemma of what to do with Sally when we are out of town was solved by Michel, my nephew. He always steps up, and volunteers to stay with the princess. He goes above and beyond by letting little

Sally sleep under the covers with him and has become our trusted Sally caretaker. He even takes photos and sends them to us while we're gone, which helps when I'm missing my girl.

The first veterinarian Sally saw when she arrived in Michigan was Dr. Jolee Wennersten in Grand Haven. I think it was love at first sight for both of them, and after nine years, Sally has seen all of the veterinarians at Robbins Road Animal Clinic at one time or another. Together we have gone through tummy aches, sprains, torn nails and a myriad of other health issues. Sally is always greeted by the staff with smiles, and she spends most of her time happy spinning in the waiting room.

With Sally's big canines, she has had her share of dental problems. Luckily, we have a fantastic doggy dentist in Dr. James Moore at Harborfront Hospital for Animals. He and his staff take excellent care of Sally's pearlies and makes sure she never has a tooth ache.

Sally's white fur is short and never needs grooming, but Ingrid with Lucky Dog Mobile Grooming keeps Sally and her brother, Eli, smelling and looking clean on a regular basis. She also tends to their nails and keeps an eye out for ear infections or health changes we might not notice. The dogs see Ingrid's mobile van coming up the driveway, and they run the other way. I don't think they consider a bath and pedicure as good things.

During the week, there are occasions where I might be gone for several hours and the dogs are inside with their furry legs crossed. I needed someone who could come over and let the dogs outside to "take care of business." Then I met student Casey Zeiler who lives around the corner. As long as she isn't wearing her flip flops - silly Sally is afraid of them - the dogs are happy to see her and I am happy knowing they are well taken care of.

There are many, many other people in our village who are important in our life with Sally, and I am grateful to everyone who has touched us in some way. This brings me to the person who encouraged me to start Life With Sally.

Writing about Sally was never even a thought until my friend Janet Vormittag asked me to write a monthly column about Sally for *Cats and Dogs Magazine*. I couldn't imagine anyone would be interested in reading stories about my dog, but five years and over 70 stories later, I was proven wrong.

My son, Jacob, told me I needed to write a book about Sally and I kept ignoring him. Then he designed the first Life With Sally book covers - and soon we had Little White Dog Tails in print. Two years later we followed with Still Spinnin' Tails, and now, with Waggin' More Tails, we have three books in the Life With Sally series.

That brings me to Sally's fans. I never thought this little white dog would ever have fans, but she does. At our first event at the PetExpo in Grand Rapids, I couldn't understand why people were lining up at our booth until I realized they were waiting for Sally's appearance. From the woman who was sending a book to her husband serving in Iraq, to the little girl who sat at the booth next to us and spent the entire day reading the book, I am so grateful and humbled by your love for my little Sally.

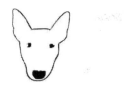

Eli Who?

Someone has to be play second fiddle to Sally, and in our house, it is Eli.

He is a jack Russell/Australian cattle dog mix and I fell in love with him the minute I saw his adoption photo in *Cats and Dogs Magazine*. No dog ever leaped out at me like Eli.

I saw my son, Jake, a few days after I saw the photo.

"I think I found our next dog," I said.

"Wait. You guys are getting another dog?" Jake asked.

"No."

"But you just said …" He raised an eye-brow at me. "Never mind," he continued. "What kind of dog?"

"His picture is in that magazine." I gestured at the magazine next to him and he started thumbing through the pages.

"That's him." Jake pointed at the photo of Eli.

"How did you know that?" I asked.

"I just know things." Jake gave me a quirky smile, which wasn't difficult for him.

And that was all it took. Well, not really, but within a couple of months, Eli was living with us and he has taken to being second-fiddle to her highness very well. But it can't be easy living in Sally's shadow.

For one thing, Sally is always going to events and Eli isn't. He gets so bummed out that now I have to put Sally outside while I ply Eli with lots (too many) of treats inside. Then I slip out the door and put Sally's harness on her in the garage, so he can't see what we are doing. He's no dummy and has figured it out. The last time this happened, I could hear him on the other side of the door whining and guilt poured onto me.

When I sit on the couch, Sally leaps up and snuggles into my left side. Eli eyes the action from the doggy pillow on the floor until I pat the couch. He jumps up to snuggle into my right side. Sally, being her jealous little self, will try to push him away and it doesn't take long before my lap is in the middle of a turf snout war. Eventually they both spread out on their official sides and ignore each other.

When we go outside together, it's all about "Sally what are you doing?" and "Sally, stop what you're doing." There is also a lot of "Sally, come here. Sally. Come. Here." She has selective hearing and quite often just ignores us. Eli, on the other hand, is very good about…what's the word? Oh yeah, behaving. When we call him, he comes – what a concept.

Many photos are taken of the little white dog, and she has even had a couple photo-shoots of her own. Not so with Eli, and he is much more cooperative when it comes to having his photo taken. Her highness tends to cooperate only when it suits her.

Wait. That is her attitude all the time, not just for photos.

Recently, I had to get a photo of Sally buckled into the car for a magazine article. I took several shots and it wasn't until later, when I was deciding which photo to use, that I spotted Eli photo-bombing from the front door.

Maybe he was trying to get his 15 minutes of fame.

About the Author

Tricia L. McDonald is no stranger to writing. As owner and operator of Splattered Ink Press (splatteredinkpress.com), Tricia has a hands-on approach to guiding others in the writing process.

As a writing coach, Tricia works one-on-one with writers to hone their writing skills, edits manuscripts, facilitates writing groups, and helps writers prepare their manuscripts for publication. As a publisher, Tricia completes the process by publishing books both in print and as eBooks.

She is an internationally published author, a public speaker and writing coach who lives and writes in West Michigan. On a volunteer basis, Tricia teaches writing classes at Four Pointes Center for Successful Aging and facilitated a class at Gilda's Club.

Her Life With Sally series: Little White Dog Tails and Still Spinnin' Tails are compilations of stories chronicling life with her miniature bull terrier, and were published in December 2009 and 2011, respectively. She also writes a monthly column, Life With Sally, for *Cats and Dogs Magazine.*

Tricia's book Quit Whining Start Writing: A Novelist's Guide to Writing (Mar 2012) is a guide to help writers put away the excuses and get the writing done. A Mind A Will A Way – The Story of John P. Harvey was published in September 2013.

Tricia has also been published in *Cup of Comfort for Mothers & Sons Anthology, The Breastfeeding Diaries Anthology, Mom Writer's Literary Magazine, Cup of Comfort for Mothers, I Love Cats Magazine* and *Oxygen Magazine.*

She is an active member of the Michigan-based writers group, Peninsula Writers, where she has coordinated yearly retreats and acts as editor of the newsletter. She is also an active member of Toastmasters International and has achieved her DTM.

Through her affiliation and work with Peninsula Writers and Toastmasters, Tricia has garnered experience organizing and presenting writing workshops, retreats and presentations.

With her compassion and humor, Tricia offers an inviting stage presence and is available for speaking events.